Radical Love

TEACHING

❧CONTEMPORARY❧

SCHOLARS

Shirley R. Steinberg
General Editor

Vol. 8

The Teaching Contemporary Scholars series is part of the Peter Lang Education list.
Every volume is peer reviewed and meets
the highest quality standards for content and production.

PETER LANG
New York • Bern • Frankfurt • Berlin
Brussels • Vienna • Oxford • Warsaw

Jesús Gómez

Radical Love

A REVOLUTION FOR THE 21ST CENTURY

Edited by Lídia Puigvert

PETER LANG
New York • Bern • Frankfurt • Berlin
Brussels • Vienna • Oxford • Warsaw

Library of Congress Cataloging-in-Publication Data

Radical love: A revolution for the 21st century /
Jesús Gómez, Lídia Puigvert (editor).
pages cm. — (Teaching contemporary scholars; vol. 8)
Includes bibliographical references and index.
1. Sexism. 2. Social perception. 3. Interpersonal relations.
4. Intimacy (Psychology) 5. Love. 6. Women—Violence against.
7. Gómez, Jesús. I. Title.
HQ1237.P85   305.3—dc23   2014016400
ISBN 978-1-4331-2650-5 (hardcover)
ISBN 978-1-4331-2649-9 (paperback)
ISBN 978-1-4539-1375-8 (e-book)
ISSN 1533-4082

Bibliographic information published by **Die Deutsche Nationalbibliothek.**
Die Deutsche Nationalbibliothek lists this publication in the "Deutsche
Nationalbibliografie"; detailed bibliographic data are available
on the Internet at http://dnb.d-nb.de/.

Cover: Small art based on a design by Ernest Alcoba
Photograph: View of Pato's beloved San Juan,
taken from the beach in Bakio, the north of Bilbao

The paper in this book meets the guidelines for permanence and durability
of the Committee on Production Guidelines for Book Longevity
of the Council of Library Resources.

© 2015 Peter Lang Publishing, Inc., New York
29 Broadway, 18th floor, New York, NY 10006
www.peterlang.com

Printed in the United States of America

*To all the boys and girls, mirrors of the future world, who experience
the awakening of their sexual-affective relationships*

Thanks to all those who collaborated in the process of translation.

Translating the book into English was not an easy task. Pato left between words his passion, the worries of the young, and a radical proposal of love. It was not only a technical job to translate this book, but also a feeling and a commitment...

We want to thank all who helped with this challenge, especially Shirley Steinberg, who worked with passion and intensity.

—Lídia Puigvert

CONTENTS

FOREWORD

Ramon Flecha

Since 1992 Jesús Gómez (Pato) understood that radical love would be the revolution of the 21st century. After millennia of oppressive societies which socialized us into desire without love for those who treat us badly and into stability without desire for those who treat us well, the theory of radical love has finally started to transform the deepest foundations of our human relations. Pato demonstrated in both his theory and his daily life that it is possible to go beyond this binary desire and mindset by "uniting affection and excitement, friendship and passion, stability and madness in the same person."

Feminist theories have already demonstrated that dominant men have always used all their power to try to keep women subdued, oppressed, and under control. The so-called double standard has been used to distinguish between two types of subordination: some women were useful for the production of the heir, and the others should be always available for sex. The new masculinities have shown that these dominant men not only oppress, subdue, and forcibly control women, but they also do so with many men. There is no doubt that Pato was in both theory and his practice one of the most revolutionary new masculinities. He lived stability and madness with terrific intensity with one of the most revolutionary feminists in theory and practice. How far he was from those men who say they are revolutionary and treat women with disdain! How far she was from those who regard themselves as feminists and yet feel desire for men who despise women! This book is not about Pato's life, but all its content is the result of the passion he put into every single moment of his existence, with an intensity that those of us who met him have never seen in any other person.

While reading these pages, readers will be reflecting about their own lives, thinking about and reliving the most important moments. But at the same time, they will be experiencing a revolution, dreaming of a much better world in each one of their own relationships.

INTRODUCTION

This book's concern with love, sex, and affective education, mainly in relation to attraction and choice, arises from the problem of gender violence, including physical and psychological violence. A friend of mine dedicated his life to discovering the causes behind all of this. According to my friend, somehow, when exploring the causes of poverty (the iceberg that we see), we find the capitalist system and its multiple ramifications, which are indeed the causes of poverty. Similarly, when examining the causes of gender violence, one has to look at the entanglement of sexual-affective relationships and the historical and socialization processes that accompany them. Once again, the tip of the iceberg (in the case of gender violence) hides the deeper and more serious problem – the system of sexual-affective relationships.

In the early 1990s, when these issues were brought to my attention, I could not even imagine that female victims of gender violence included not only women who were financially dependent on their husbands but also university students who were victimized by their partners or casual lovers. However, I had to admit these facts after an increasing number of cases came to light. I learned that as a result of the established traditional model of relationships (with centuries of history behind it), many women victims of gender violence were not only financially and emotionally dependent on their abusers but also wished to continue these destructive relationships. I would have preferred to be able to refute this evidence. I would have also preferred to disprove the fact that some of these women victims reported that the best sexual intercourse occurred after a fight. However, such evidence was clear and appears in research each day. Our society, aptly named the Risk Society, has generated many advantages, but it has also aggravated the precarious system of sexual-affective relationships.

Based on my friend's suggestion, we surfed television channels to determine how many of the men who drive women wild in bed in different films are those who also change their child's diapers and how many of these men are actively involved in violent situations. Then, we examined teenage magazines to determine whether good boys or aggressive boys are presented as more attractive. My friend also suggested that we interview adolescents and focus on the sort of boys they talk about with sexual desire and the type of boys they talk about only in a friendly way. He stated that although people in stable or casual partnerships may not be touched by the socialization of a desire for violence, this desire is currently the dominant model of sexuality in our society, which is marked by sexism. My friend claimed that it is another case of the "tip of the iceberg" and thus reports are increasing of gender violence among financially independent young people who are viewed as liberals and even feminists within their environment.

Then, I began to hear about more serious cases at earlier ages. Blow by blow, a world that I was unaware of, although it was close to me, began to appear. I became convinced of the truth of a statement that my friend repeatedly professed: if we do not transform ourselves so as not to be attracted to perpetrators of gender violence, then we will never eliminate it. If chauvinists and perpetrators of gender violence continue to be more successful in affective and sexual relationships than egalitarian and nice people, then the situation will not change and will only grow worst.

In one case, a 12-year-old girl refused to return to school. She had performed acts of masturbation on six of her male classmates. She enjoyed the first experience but felt forced into it. However, she believed that she would look bad in front of the boy and her classmates if she refused. The other male classmates approached her with the assumption that she would also do the same to them. She even boasted that the boys who were most desired by her friends were chasing after her. Her teachers and parents were not aware of the situation. One day, her mother returned from the supermarket and stated that the mother of one of the six boys thought that her son had a crush on the girl based on hearing him talk about her to a friend. Shortly thereafter, one of the girl's friends began dating one of the six boys. From that point forward, all of the girl's friends stopped talking to her, stating that she was a whore. She could not handle the situation and refused to return to school. When the headmistress was informed about the situation, she exclaimed, "It's just kids' stuff."

Given these hidden situations in our daily lives and the realization that teachers and family members can be as misled as I used to be, I asked myself the following questions: Why do we feel attracted to certain people, and who satisfies our need to attract? Who do we like and why? Who do we choose and why? Who do we attract, and who chooses us? The answers to these questions reflect the basis of our current model of attraction and choice.

This book was written in the Department of Methods of Research and Diagnosis in Education of the University of Barcelona and also in the Center for Research on Theory and Practices for Overcoming Inequalities (CREA). In CREA, I discovered a great degree of concern for and scientific dedication to the Center's goals thanks to a serious line of research on the preventive socialization of gender violence as well as a communicative methodology with a considerable international impact. In the department of Research and Diagnostic Methods in Education, I discovered rigorous work on research methodologies and unanimous scientific and human support during difficult times. My work there provided empirical evidence that another world and other types of sexual-affective relationships are possible.

This book deals with a field in which science is conspicuously absent and superstition reigns. One hears such expressions as "love is blind"; it is "chemistry"; "it hits you like lightning"; "it comes and goes like a thief without warning"; and "a couple's passion lasts for a maximum of 18 to 36 months" as well as many other misconceptions and old wives' tales. Scientific knowledge that is linked to sexual-affective relationships is vital and must be incorporated into the educational process. The social repercussions of misinformation are substantial, as it is a subject that affects all people.

A first kiss or a first romance that is innocent, loving, devoted, and involves two young people who love each other is not comparable to an experience in which an individual feels used as a means to another's ends. In the latter experience, the user has no real interest in the individual, although he/she attempts to convince the individual otherwise. Giving yourself to someone, feeling that the person you are madly in love with is also madly in love with you, is completely the opposite of the discomfort associated with knowing that someone no longer needs you after their own objective has been achieved. In addition, history often repeats itself, proving the following famous proverb: "Man is the only animal to trip over the same stone twice."

How does love work? Can a person be in love and still control his or her behavior in a rational manner? Does something have to happen to that person in a "spontaneous" way? Do people need to subconsciously seek fathers and mothers in their romantic relationships? Does attraction have to have the sole aim of reproducing the human species? Is there a universal law of human nature that creates an inverse association between passion and reason? Do we have to hopelessly "fall" into the arms of the conqueror? Our sexual-affective lives and all associated factors largely depend on the type of people we fall in love with, those who attract us, and those who we do not want to give up. Torment, apathy, or satisfaction will result from relationships based on passion without love, love without passion, or loving passion, respectively.

In fact, a transcendental aspect will escape us if we do not carry out an in-depth exploration of the reasons behind all of these aspects. Thus, I will analyze sexual-affective relationships in society today. Although the theoretical bases provided can be applied to people of any age, research examined whether adolescents in relationships act according to the traditional and conservative model or according to an alternative model based on progressive values.

We searched for elements of change that allow for the possibility of improving relationships; theories and/or practices that generate both satisfactory attraction as well as satisfactory choice and a suitable model for sexual-affective relationships. The fundamental objective was not only to determine who attracts us, who we attract, who we choose, and who chooses us (specifically, their values) but also how we can change those aspects that negatively affect us.

As anthropology grows in importance, we hope this book will be used as an extension of sociology, psychology, and education. It contains new elements that contribute to overcoming the barriers that have impeded the study of attraction and choice in the area of love. These elements also help to overcome superstitions by replacing hypotheses that view love and attraction as "instinct," "chemistry," for those based on the history of interactions and the identity constitution within intersubjective decision-making dynamics. Love, attraction, and choice are aspects of a book that we must write on the basis of consensus and the definition of our own rules.

This book is divided into five chapters. The first three chapters contain reflections on theories of choice and attraction, contemporary love, and sexual-affective relationship models. The last two chapters contain reflections on practice (including the voices of adolescents), conclusions, and the outlook for the future.

The first chapter addresses key aspects that have received little attention. Following a discussion of socialization, attraction and choice-related theories are reviewed. This task leads us to the fields of psychology and sociology as well as to references to biology and the extensive range of literature in this area. Beck and Beck-Gernsheim (1995), Giddens (1993), and Sternberg (1998) are quoted in the field of attraction. The works of Elster (1999, 2000), Habermas (1987a, 1987b), and other philosophers as well as writers of literature and essayists such as Ortega y Gasset (1999) are compulsory reading in the area of choice. The following areas are highlighted: (1) socialization, as the values with which we are socialized leave a deep impression in terms of our preferences, tastes, attraction, choice, and desire in love. (2) The disturbing lack of scientific research in the field of attraction, which is examined through the folklore that "the inevitable [just] happens" or is based on instinct, "chemistry," or biology, and so on. (3) The benefits of placing the focus on intersubjectivity as the communicative route that leads to the best results.

The second chapter contains an exhaustive review of contemporary theories on love through an analysis of the work and theories of the most significant authors. These works include Giddens's *The Transformation of Intimacy* (1993), Luhmann's *Liebe als Passion* [*Love as Passion*] (1986), and Beck and Beck-Gernsheim's *The Normal Chaos of Love* (1995). In addition, we emphasize the psychological aspects of Sternberg's *Love Is a Story: A New Theory of Relationships* (1998). According to the results of this analysis, we can see new opportunities to develop satisfactory sexual-affective relationships based on four key components: modernity and its radicalization, the prominence of social actors, the role of dialogue and consensus, and re-enchantment in the area of communication. The formula for a transformative approach to love lies in these components.

The third chapter, grounded in the theoretical reflections in the two previous chapters, examines two models of sexual-affective relationships – the traditional model and an alternative model. We analyze the foundations of the first model, together with the elements that have traditionally shaped each gender's features and then transmitted and introduced them into society. The three classic variations of this model are womanizers, women who imitate that masculine model, and stable but passionless couples. Furthermore, we demonstrate that most prominent social sciences authors continue to use this traditional model. As for the second model, we describe its basic qualities and then develop a profile in which stability and passion occur at the same time and with the same person.

The fourth chapter contains the voices of the adolescent participants. We examine whether, due to coeducation and contemporary critical practices, adolescents' attraction and subsequent choices are governed by the new model of relationships. In other words, we test whether adolescents continue to be governed by the traditional model. The analysis of the collected[1] material allows us to reach initial conclusions concerning the type of people who we are attracted to, how we are socialized in the area of love, and the values of those persons we like or choose. We can then create a suitable response to this basic question: Do we feel attraction to and choose according to the traditional model or to an alternative model?

The fifth and final chapter contains conclusions and criticisms that are linked to the models (the traditional and the alternative ones) and indicates the gaps in theories and critical educational proposals. The key points of the alternative model are emphasized. In the future, the development of an educational model and some basic competences that can place adequate knowledge within our reach may help us to feel attraction and choose based on transformative values.

· 1 ·

ATTRACTION AND CHOICE THEORIES AND CHOICE IN SEXUAL-AFFECTIVE RELATIONSHIPS

An analysis of relationships in our society cannot be based on the fantastic opportunities that emerge or are missed. Rather, it must be based on which model people follow on a daily basis when relating to others. In other words, such an analysis must be based on whether we are guided by the traditional model, which is based on the values embodied by previous societies and traditional teaching, or by an alternative model in which the progressive keys to current society and a coeducational philosophy prevail.

Prior to model creation, we must analyze the two key processes that sexual-affective relationships are based on: attraction and choice. Although these processes are firmly interwoven, they must be pried apart and analyzed individually. We need to understand the ways in which we are socialized about relationships and the values that we internalize through the family, school's sex and affective education, and other agents (basically, the media). We must recognize the available opportunities to choose and how they are utilized. Without a thorough analysis of all these factors, relationships and relationship models would be meaningless. I hope that the development of the different attraction and choice theories will allow us to not only understand human desires and behavior but also to create the necessary relationship models.

Socialization occurs throughout life, and people internalize the values and social norms of the culture in which they live. However, socialization does not determine behavior, as the individual always makes the final determination. What is of interest then is that final determination on which our subsequent actions depend. We must have a clear understanding of what is guiding us. Is it what we say, what we do, or what we would like to do?

This subject leads me to examine such questions as: Is love instinctive? Is it chemistry, social influence, or a combination of various factors? Which people attract us? Why? What about them attracts us? These questions tend to be avoided but must be answered in order to clarify why some people choose either persons who hurt and break their dreams or other persons who will mean stability but not passion. Let me pay attention here to the most important (as well as most ignored) issue: attraction. I inspect certain definitions of love and its related considerations as well as the personalities of people who conquer and of those who suffer. In this investigation, I reference such authors as Beck and Beck-Gernsheim (1995), Freud (1975), Fromm (1959), Giddens (1993), Lee (1988), Ortega y Gasset (1999), and Sternberg (1998). As demonstrated throughout this book, the basis of satisfactory relationships can be found in our tastes, preferences, desires, and attractions as well as in our ability to change these characteristics when they prove detrimental.

Finally, I analyze the last step before establishing a relationship: choice. For this analysis, I conduct an in-depth examination of the work of two key authors in this area. Jon Elster (1999, 2000, 2001) is well known for the theory and treatment of rational choice, but his strong point is his study of emotions and what is considered irrational behavior. Jurgen Habermas's theory of communicative action (1987a, 1987b) led to a new direction in the social sciences and and is useful in our discussion of choice.

Socialization

Prior to the analysis of attraction and choice, I introduce the subject of socialization, which should be analyzed in greater depth at this point. In fact, people have been aware for a long time that love responds to pre-established factors (Ortega y Gasset, 1999: 32).

Berger and Luckmann (1968) define socialization as the process that people undergo to first become members of society and then to be led into new sectors of the world. According to these authors, the creation of the "generalized other" within consciousness is fundamental, as it involves the internalization of society and its objective reality while also establishing identity in a subjective manner. The world that is internalized in the socialization process penetrates most strongly during the early years, basically through language.

Although these authors discussed primary and secondary socialization (Berger and Luckmann, 1968), society no longer makes this distinction because socialization is carried out as a continuous process throughout life. We cannot state that school and the family represent primary socialization and that the media and the peer group perform to secondary socialization, as, for example, very young children may spend many hours watching television. The virtual world has been incorporated into our lives, and the Internet is increasingly becoming another member of the family. Berger and Luckmann not only examined the inevitable socialization, they also noted the opportunity for great transformations ("alternations"), which require processes of resocialization (religious conversion is an excellent example).

Our current focus is how we can resocialize after a damaging sexual-affective socialization. Rather than discussing a social basis to be used as "laboratory" for transformation, we must "deprogram" ourselves of the traditional values that we have internalized and simultaneously "reprogram" ourselves with new progressive values, something nearly impossible to achieve as an individual.

In addition to examining theories on girls' and boys' development,[1] Giddens (1993) briefly analyzed the agencies of socialization and resocialization. With regard to socialization, the most influential position is that of the family (primarily the mother), which currently takes on a variety of forms. As the child grows older, he/she is then influenced by the peer group (especially when it is a strong group), the school, where children learn basic roles, and the media, which have acquired a great deal of significance. With regards to resocialization, Giddens exclusively discussed extreme, critical situations without tackling the sexual-affective area. He refers to resocialization processes as the disruption of previously accepted values and patterns of behavior followed by the adoption of radically different ones (Giddens, 1993b: 80), such as the changes of personality undergone by the prisoners in concentration camps or the behavior of individuals suffering brainwashing practices.

Current analysis focuses on the relationships that are influenced by socializing processes that condition both attraction and choice. For example, suppose two opposites that are theoretically irreconcilable, such as violence versus love or desire versus attraction to violence, become united due to the strong force of socialization. In short, this connection can only harm us.

There are numerous examples of love-punishment in families and between people who "love" each other ("those who love you will make you cry"[2]). However, the most extreme situations take place in the media, especially in television programs and films in which the "hot guy" is violent. Nearly all young boys, when thinking about their future, wish to emulate the hero who resolves problems, and little girls wish to be the beautiful woman who falls into the arms of the hero. Later, we witness aggressive relationships, which many girls become hooked on. In these cases, we either do not wish to understand why this occurs or search for explanations of a biological or psychoanalytical nature. However, it may be more productive to examine and intervene in certain socialization processes that show many centuries of history in a harsh light. For example, families and schools can choose pathways based on dialogue, respect, and the freedom of choice and equality between men and women. However, few people attempt to determine whether adolescents choose according to these values or to more traditional guidelines in their first sexual-affective relationships.

Where are these guidelines best represented? Who reproduces and "educates" according to these guidelines? Why do we choose the most popular ones rather than those with better values? If we wish to improve our sexual-affective relationships, it is vital to examine how, why, and who we choose. A correct choice can promote socialization in accordance with positive values, whereas a bad choice may diminish the effects of the best values received.

Attraction in relationships

For centuries, we have accumulated images of "graceful femininity" and "strong and powerful men," of the rejection of women who dress like men, perform "men's jobs," or participate in typical "male sports," and are not concerned about looking pretty. We have always rejected men who carry out activities that have traditionally been considered to be more female oriented, such as mopping, cleaning, or changing a child's diaper. The refrain is well known: "It's men's stuff" or "women's stuff." Attraction has also been guided by that same refrain.

Instead of considering (and possibly rejecting) the values of the person we desire, we may just prefer to "fall" into that person's arms in a way that appears to be involuntary and impossible to predict. Many proverbs and folk sayings are often used to justify this attitude – "if someone attracts you, there must be a reason behind it"; "everyone knows that love is blind," etc. However, before reaching any conclusions, I analyze certain considerations in the area of attraction.

Social basis and attraction theories

Is attraction instinct, "chemistry," social influence, or a mixture of all three? This difficult and complicated question caused Giddens to ask: "Why can't a good man be sexy and why can't a sexy man be good? This is a plea from the heart, not just a quixotic feminine refusal to accept the full implications of gender equality" (Giddens, 1993: 156).

We do not agree with Giddens's statement. A "plea from the heart" is another reference to biology, instinct, or chemistry. What exactly is the heart? Giddens appears to refer to values that have been internalized over many years that the individual who dominates, is a leader, makes decisions, and despises people is desirable He also appears to refer to the values that define men who are kind, give themselves to others, and place themselves in positions of equality as unattractive. A discussion of "the heart" is unjustified unless it states that this question "from the heart" is the result of a certain social influence and indicates the type of influence exerted. If emotion and motivation are inseparable and the latter is rational (such that it can be objectified), the dilemma lies in how to define the socialization that guides both motivation and the lack of it, change this motivation, and transform, I would say, "what comes out from within." This process, which I consider fundamental to the development of a love life, is lacking in Giddens's work.

On the other hand, when analyzing the evolution of loving relationships toward increased democracy, Giddens viewed unmarried couples, married couples, and families in terms of the following alternatives: (1) one in which the home serves as simply the shared "headquarters" for the occupants who have independent lives or (2) one in which the home contains a relationship based on friendship and affection that lacks passion. If we teach progressive values but our desires are driven by traditional values, we create turbulent relationships and/or endorse Giddens's images of either a "headquarters-home" or an affectionate relationship lacking passion. If ethics do not coincide with our desires but we act in accordance with them, if socialization is based on how we live and not on how we would like to live, and if the people who we spend time with, desire, dream and fantasize about have values that are the opposite of those recommended through education, then what type of future are we creating? Are we preparing a gift that will never be unwrapped? Or are we preparing a beautifully wrapped, hermetically sealed box of values that is locked with the key of demotivation?

Beck and Beck-Gernsheim (1995) considered love to be a triumph of modernity and believed that humans are today able to enjoy some freedom and equality in the midst of the chaos of love. According to their view of the individualization process (involuntary rather than causal and neither desired nor based on knowledge), attraction cannot be improved: "It simply happens, strikes like lightning or dies out according to laws which are not open to individual or social control" (Beck and Beck-Gernsheim, 1995: 198).

Although these authors tackled the problem and took successful risks, even in their intuitions, they did not provide an in-depth investigation into the questions of who we like, why and how we like them, or the real socialization processes. Therefore, they believed that attraction is impossible to manage or stop because love hits an individual like lightning and departs in the same manner. This idea was also expressed by Ortega y Gasset (1999), who blamed "the machine of preferring and disdaining" – the heart. Similarly, in a sign from the heart, Giddens (1993) viewed the good guy and the sexy guy as opposites. Considering biology, instinct, or "chemistry" rather than the social question is a mistake in that it justifies the worst sexual-affective relationships.

Concerning attraction theories, the psychological point of view (which tends to be accompanied by the biological rationale when a plausible explanation cannot be found), Sternberg (1998) provided a brief overview. Among these theories, he underlined the theory of reactance in the psychological literature. According to this theory, it is natural to desire a person who is hard to get and to dispose of him/her once he/she has been attracted: "There is, though, an irony in all this. After basking in the glory of being 'unique,' some of these people come to feel their freedom [is] being threatened and to worry about being rushed into a commitment. They begin to withdraw and the relationship ends. What works in the short term may backfire in the long term" (Sternberg, 1998: 121). Thus, he attempted to justify a typical situation using his theory. According to Sternberg, once the prey is captured, the person who flirts abandons the prey and may despise and humiliate him/her. This notion is examined – and strongly criticized – in greater detail in Chapter 3, in which we analyze the traditional sexual-affective attraction-choice relationship model. Furthermore, Sternberg continues, "Reactance theory has an interesting implication for why couples who live together before marriage are no more likely to stay together after marriage than are couples who do not first [live] together (...). When a couple lives together without marriage, there may be psychological commitments, but there is no legal one, and either member of the couple who disagrees with the psychological commitments is always free to leave. Marriage can generate a state of reactance" (1998: 121–122). However, one may ask why two people who lived together for several years without getting married eventually do so. If the answer is that the couple ran out of passion and motivation and believed – consciously or subconsciously – that getting married would solve the problem, then it is possible to understand their subsequent separation, as marriage can only sustain that situation for a short time. In the same vein, the decision to bear children to bring more life into a relationship is not reactance. Rather, it is an attempt to "escape through moving forward" in a relationship that lost its meaning.

In line with the considerable research that has been carried out in this area, Sternberg discussed the way that we tend to choose people who are similar to us. Yela and Sangrador (2001) concluded that we tend to fall in love with people who have the same level of attractiveness that we do, although we view the other person as somewhat more attractive. With time, a decrease in attractiveness is compensated by an increase in familiarity, cognitive dissonance, and so on. With regards to these tendencies in relation to falling in love and the strength of power to seduce women and beauty to captivate men, we claim that this research should incorporate some analysis of the difficulties of pairing up with a person who stands out due to power or beauty. In other words, we must determine whether we fall in love with similar people or people who are complementary to us because we are strongly attracted to them or because those who we most desire do not choose us. Furthermore, we should determine who we desire for sporadic relationships (e.g., "one-night stands") and those we choose for stable relationships. If these do not coincide, then we must deeply reflect on this and understand why statements such as "he's so hot" or "she's so attractive" are not necessarily associated with people with whom one should want to spend one's life.

Finally, some psychoanalytical theories are incapable of answering simple questions like why the same people attract people who are very different. These theories include those of Freud (1975), who considers love as sublimated sexuality; of Klein and Riviere (1953), who view love as dependence on other people to satisfy one's own needs; of Maslow (1975), who considers the shortcomings of love as deriving from the need to belong and feel secure; and of Fromm (1947, 1959), who analyzes the fear of freedom and the art of loving. In Lee's (1988) often-cited six styles of loving, the author attempts to characterize the different forms of loving by mixing attraction with choice. However, he does not provide an in-depth examination of who we are attracted to and why. It is somewhat symptomatic that he does not consider the possibility of a love that is both passionate and stable.

The concept of the divorce between passion-craziness and affection-stability is widespread. In fact, it has nearly become a mathematical axiom. Thus, authors such as Altable (1998) posit that passion is suffering, a rage, insanity, a disorder, a factor that causes a loss of rationality, a hope, an affliction, a shiver, and a desire to melt that is never satisfied (which is why it increases as the object of desire becomes farther away). Furthermore, such authors claim that passion causes an individual to feel unhappy or at least unsatisfied. Passion becomes profound envy of that which is unreachable and desirable. Thus, it goes hand in hand with inequality and generates devotion and self-abandonment. With regard to the romantic conception of love, Altable (1998) insisted that women do not know how to navigate the situation. Specifically, as soon as the other approaches because he feels attracted to her, he then retreats because he is afraid of loving her or depending on her as he depended on his mother. Thus, he feels a need to control her.

In fact, the other's movement (as is demonstrated in Chapter 3, in which we tackle the traditional relationship model) is linked to other issues, such as centuries of accumulated tradition and socialization rather than to the romantic concept of love and the fear of depending on the woman. Likewise, passion does not need to be connected to a disorder or envy. And it does not necessarily increase when the object of desire is far away. Because people are unable to explain the mechanisms of attraction, they invent reasons that are typically of a biological or psychoanalytical nature.

In short, there is a dearth of authors and theories that delve deeper into the subject of attraction in sexual-affective relationships, so we lack knowledge in this area. The knowledge we do have is limited to disciplines such as sociology, psychology, and biology. Incursions into philosophy have been made, and literature is the most fruitful, although the least scientific and systematic, area. Books and articles in top journals discuss flirting and attraction, although they only reflect certain facts, preferences, and techniques without delving deeper into the subject. In addition, some books state that jealousy is as necessary as love and sex (Buss, 2000). Other books view love as a game and provide certain rules to follow to find love (Carter-Scott, 1999). Some authors justify the relationship between love and hate, violence and admiration, and attraction and repulsion (Salecl, 1998). Others teach girls to love bad boys, how to live with them, and when to leave them (Lieberman, 1997). Certain authors consider seduction as communication or deceit (Bercovich, 1996), and some describe sexual chemistry and how to use it (Fast, 1983). There are also articles on boys who find pleasure in seducing virgins and then lose interest the following day, "playboys," and the difficulty of saying "no" (Deniega, 1995). These articles also include the idea that cognitive jealousy is a positive for relationships (Dugosh, 2000); that young, aggressive men are considered very attractive (Bukowski, Sippola, and Newcomb, 2000); and that adulation, ideal love, and romantic love are the three stages of attraction (Kemper and Reid, 1997). Other ideas include abstinence as a method of saving passion (Dorno, 1993); the biological theory of the effect of hormones on adolescent sexual behavior (Udry, 1988); and the anthropological viewpoint of lust and attraction as different emotions related to brain chemistry (McDonald, 1998). There is also the evolutionary theory that incorporates the biological and neurological elements involved in love while basing sexual attraction on natural selection (Norman, 1998).

A significant problem is that the authors of the above-mentioned books and articles discuss certain characteristics that are linked to attraction without asking certain fundamental social questions before reaching their conclusions. Therefore, the analyses demonstrate a lack of depth. A typical example is in any study on how long passion lasts in sexual-affective relationships. All of them state that passion decreases over time in such a way that it lasts for roughly 18 to 36 months. Thus, the researcher deduces that passion evidences this cycle, and then biological data, such as certain hormones, substances, and bodily reactions, are added to the text. In short, we are told not to worry about passion disappearing from our relationships because that is practically inevitable. However, if these investigations aimed at understanding where this lack of motivation comes from by citing such factors as routine and habits, having achieved what was desired, a lack of communication, a lack of freedom, and, fundamentally, the ideas that good boys are weak and girls lose their beauty, their conclusions would differ. Specifically, the results would be attributed to social issues. If such issues are taken into account, the loss of passion can be reversed so that relationships can maintain or increase passion over time.

Another common misconception concerns jealousy and love. There is no scientific weight behind the statement that lovers are jealous people or that great love entails searing jealousy. On the contrary, we should analyze love and jealousy as two conflicting emotions. Overall, there is a dearth of work that conducts an in-depth analysis of the underlying mechanisms or thoroughly discusses the subject with the aim of understanding the long history and strength of the traditional model of attraction.

The conqueror and the sufferer

The classic model of traditional attraction depicts certain historical roles with great precision – the person who conquers and the person who is the object of that conquest. The conqueror to whom women are madly attracted (on the one hand) and the woman who suffers (on the other hand) appear in an abundant amount of written material, including major works of world literature and magazine and/or newspaper articles. This does not minimize the fact that the roles of the male "sufferer" and female "conqueror" were also prevalent. However, assuming this role of conqueror does not satisfactorily resolve modern women's attempts to achieve authentic liberation. In fact, it is a mere reversal of the *traditional model of masculinity*,[3] namely, of the classic and unsatisfactory relationship that is the cause of many affective and sexual dramas.

This issue is so assimilated that the link between passion and suffering is considered natural. This model has been employed in important works of literature since ancient times. It can be observed in Hebbel's tragedy *Genoveva* and the letters of Mariana Alcoforado, which reflect the masochism often attributed to women in literature.[4]

And then there is Chateaubriand (speaking from the other side), who inspired the following enlightening comments: "A man who – incapable of feeling true love – has had the gift of awakening authentic loves (…) **suddenly and forever.**" Chateaubriand would have forcefully devised a doctrine in which never dying and being born suddenly would be essential to true love (…) Stendhal believes – this is consistent with his experience – that love is "made" and that, additionally, it ends. Both attributes are characteristic of pseudo-love. Chateaubriand, on the other hand, always finds love "made." He does not need to toil (…) These are not fantasies: they are documented facts (Ortega y Gasset, 1999: 81, 84, 85).

This attraction, which makes us suffer and is essential to the sadistic and masochistic processes, gave birth to what Freud called the Thanatos, or the death instinct. The father of psychoanalysis was not able to find reasonable explanations for such destructive and self-destructive behavior and, thus, created a new instinct to justify it. However, with the same lack of success, Ortega y Gasset describes the role of the heart:

> The heart, a machine of preference and disdain, is what supports our personality. Before we know what surrounds us we launch ourselves at it from different directions, towards some values or others (…) our heart, with the obstinacy of the stars, one feels appointed to a predetermined orbit. (Ortega y Gasset, 1999: 133–141)

The philosopher could not explain why the wrong people attract us. Thus, he stated that the heart is a machine of preference and disdain and that our interior is neither rational nor free.

Of the three great sociologists who specifically studied love in recent years (Beck, Giddens, and Luhmann), Giddens is the only one who addressed the subject of womanizers: "Some such men have sex with a hundred or more women a year (…) His dependence upon women therefore, can only be validated through the mechanics of sexual conquest (…) The womanizer appears as a figure who 'loves them and leaves them.' In fact, he is quite unable to leave them: each leaving is only the prelude to another encounter" (Giddens, 1993: 84–85).

He also stated that some womanizers seize the hearts of women and that nearly all of them are willing to become deeply involved in a relationship once they have begun it. Likewise, he warned that before the relationship begins, codependent women realize – partly unconsciously – that their devotion will be rejected (1993).

According to Giddens (1993), the womanizer both feels dependent on women and loves them. We will criticize this position later, but at this point we simply express our disagreement. Womanizers do not seek profound relationships. In addition, codependent women are aware of womanizers' intentions. Because attraction is easy to observe but difficult to explain, Giddens did not find a solution but provided a justification for these tastes, preferences, and behavior. Subsequently, Giddens sometimes appealed to irrationality (heart matters are simply "like that") and other times employed a psychoanalytic approach.

We have seen, mainly through Sternberg's works (1998), how psychological theories analyze attraction in terms of what is difficult to achieve and use such words as "similarity," "complementarity," "sequential filter," "value-role stimulus," and "dyadic education," and also employ practical theories. If we only deeply examine what attracts us (as if it were inevitable) and ignore the reasons behind attraction, as is typically the case, then psychoanalysis is most helpful. This perspective attempts to respond to behavior that involves a male conqueror and a female who suffers because of her relationship with him, perhaps because she is seeking, for example, the love of a dominant father figure. The situation may also involve female codependence, male dependence, and so on.

However, in attempting to free themselves from the chains of a patriarchal society, some women have imitated the traditional model of masculinity with negative consequences. This results in constant dissatisfaction because an oppressive model cannot provide satisfactory sexual-affective relationships. However, in this case, psychoanalysis is seriously constrained. How can it explain the female conqueror? Once again, a suitable response will not be found without delving deeper into social influence, as history indicates the different types of behavior in the domain of attraction and choice.

Choice in relationships

In our society, the opportunities to choose and the obligation to do so are being developed daily. The main issue is not what we feel about a certain type of person or why we are attracted to those with the worst values. Rather, the issue involves decisions that we cannot avoid: Who do we choose? Do we allow ourselves to be led by the "irrationality" of our hearts? Or do we follow what is dictated to us by reason? Or do we follow a combination of both? What theories exist in this area, and which is the most suitable?

In introducing the most prominent theories on choice, we exclude those that we examined in the section on attraction, as they addressed both attraction and choice. Therefore, my current theoretical framework will be linked to two important authors, Elster (1996, 1999, 2000, 2001) and Habermas (1987a, 1987b). In the discussion on attraction, we noted the dearth of research on the role of social development. By contrast, in regard to choice, both authors (particularly Habermas) address the need to incorporate interaction into the process of choice, allowing for a transformative dialogue.

The theory of rational choice, social norms, and emotions

Elster (1996) summarized the theory of rational choice by stating that people (faced with the opportunity to choose between alternatives) do what they think will provide them with a better, more satisfactory overall result.

However, in relation to love, when we choose based on attraction, we move far away from rational choice, which is based on instrumental rationality.

With some choices, we cause and endure such damage that we seem to be irrational beings. Elster (1999) was concerned with emotions because they represent people's fundamental and irrational aspects, which often act as a guide beyond rational considerations. As observed, Giddens (1993), Ortega y Gasset (1999), and Beck and Beck-Gernsheim (1995), among other authors, believed that there is something which cannot be avoided or predicted (the heart's desire, the lightning strike, etc.). Thus, Elster (2000) discussed other influences that may counter rational choice, such as social norms and emotions.

At times, choices, which are the precursors to acts, are oriented toward fulfilling social norms rather than seeking the greatest personal benefits. On other occasions, emotions ("irrationality") serve as guides. We can observe these phenomena either as effects produced by various causes or as causes that produce certain effects.

Elster distinguished between simple or basic emotions and complex and profound emotions. Examples of the former are sexual desire, hate, fear, and paternal/maternal emotions and are generated by perceptions which can be understood according to evolution theories. Complex emotions include jealousy, envy, revenge, anger, and indignation, which are only typical of humans and are generated by complex and subtle beliefs. However, as independent variables, emotions interfere with the formation of rational beliefs. They reduce the rationality of our beliefs, as they lead us to act quickly, and affect rational choice, as they narrow the focus of attention and can have somatic consequences (even a heart attack).

In line with Elster, I recognize the significance of emotions but note one discrepancy in his theory. Specifically, he stated that sexual desire is a basic emotion because any animal could have it. However, it seems clear that it creates a social question that is typical of the human race and therefore is a complex emotion. Eating is a biological need (if we do not eat, we die), and fear, when facing danger in nature (an avalanche, which may fall on us, or a boa constrictor, which may attack us), is a basic emotion. However, sexual desire has its origins in social need (we can live and even reproduce our species without this desire through the genetic advances that have taken place) and I, thus, include it among the other profound emotions. Because it is socially grounded, sexual desire can be addressed and transformed through interaction, a consideration that is highly significant in regard to the topic here.

When they originate from complex beliefs, emotions generate actions that cannot be explained by the theory of rational choice and do not necessarily adjust to social norms. The humanities provide a greater array of these effects than does any scientific field. Although we have some understanding of the neurophysiology of emotions and perceptions, we lack knowledge about the neurophysiology of complex beliefs. Therefore, we search the works of novelists and poets rather than scientists. Elster (1999, 2000) stated that fear, hate, friendship, and love have double effects. On the one hand, they motivate with overwhelming strength. On the other hand, they distort our point of view.

Thus, we may not operate to our own benefit in these situations. However, Elster took a critical stand and overcame the commonly accepted direct opposition of human rationality and "natural emotion": "A person who is passionately in love may remain perfectly lucid about his prospects and in full control of his behavior (…) There is no universal law of human nature expressing an inverse relation between passion and reason" (Elster, 2000: 158).

Elster also looked at the situation in the communicative perspective. He demonstrated that in addition to choosing according to preferences, dialogue is held, arguments are provided, pacts are made, and consensus is reached along the lines set out by Habermas (1987a, 1987b). Deliberative democracy (Elster, 2000) has led to adjustments in his theory, providing the following panorama in terms of choice.

Rational choice

We choose what we believe to be best for us based on our own interests. We want to reach an end, and we use all necessary means to achieve that end. If we wish to live with a person who provides us with security, has money, and is a good person, we will use every means within our reach to find an individual who matches these characteristics and to make him or her fall in love with us.

Choice based on social norms

We choose by following the norms of our social group, whether the choice is in our best interests or not. Social pressure and/or pressure from the peer group can be quite strong. If having relationships with the most socially valued people (possibly those who have had the greatest number of relationships without any loving feelings) is viewed as desirable or linked to success in our group of friends, we will most likely search for the people who meet these criteria.

Choice that is dependent on emotions

We choose according to the motivating and distorting strength of our emotions, regardless of rationality and social norms. This is the most astonishing case. The authors who tackle this subject (as well as the media) believe that falling in love is an irresistible emotion that causes people suffering and joy. According to this approach, if we "fall" into the trap of love, we have already "chosen." I advise readers to take note of Elster's quote above concerning the nonuniversality of the inverse relationship between passion and reason.

Choice through intersubjectivity

Dialogue allows us to reach a consensus and choose the option that we believe is most appropriate. Elster, through the evolution of his discourse, moves toward the possibility of changing any choice (rational, social, or emotional) if necessary. However, he has not yet adopted a definitive position in the communicative perspective.

Theory of communicative action as applied to choice

I complement this theoretical framework with Habermas's (1987a, 1987b) theory of communicative action as applied to choice in sexual-affective relationships. According to Habermas, choice (1) is instrumental or oriented to individual goals, (2) follows the social norms, (3) relates to the image that we wish to portray ("the theatre of life"), or (4) is communicative or based on intersubjective dialogue in search for agreement between the people involved.

Habermas defended communicative rationality, which allows people to choose while gathering the rulings of the objective world and following the intersubjectivity guidelines of the context. In general, arguments are required, and these arguments require validity claims. That is, for a choice to be considered good, it cannot be imposed by force. Rather, a dialogue in which the strength of the arguments prevails over power-based arguments must be initiated. Below, we focus on the three most important validity claims (Habermas, 1987a) and their forms of argumentation.

Truth claims (true or false)

Such claims are evident in the field of science. Arguments intend to convince people on a universal level. If strong arguments are provided, it can be demonstrated (for example) that a specific type of person always makes others fall in love with him/her and then despises them once they are "captured."

Rightness claims (good or bad)

These claims are found in the field of morals. Arguments with the same intention are provided. It can be demonstrated that the behavior that certain individuals always display (courtship and conquest, then disdain) is morally unacceptable. This moral view concerns both the behavior and the impact that it has on those who are humiliated.

Claims or standards of value (pretty or ugly)

These claims belong in the field of aesthetics. Although it is worthwhile to exchange impressions and hold debates, there is no need to reach agreement, as the standards are a matter of taste.

Now we are able to discuss the four types of action (Habermas, 1987a), which represent choices.

1. Teleological

We choose the best means to reach an end. We run the risk of making a mistake because we must choose among alternatives. Using an example of rational choice, if we wish to live with an individual who provides us with security, has a significant amount of money, and falls in love with us, we must choose among the people who meet these requirements. One variant of this choice is the strategic choice, in which other people's decisions are also considered. This type of action suggests that we make calculations based upon what those people are likely thinking and the steps that they will predictably take (e.g., who will choose us, what they will expect of us, how they will behave, and what their reactions will be to our actions).

2. Normatively regulated

We choose according to the norms of our social world, with the group that we belong to or our peer group selecting the pathway for us to follow. Along these lines, we might live with good people who provide us with security and have a good social position because this is considered acceptable in our group. But suppose first we had considered living with people who attract us much more, people who are "conquerors" and would cause us to suffer. We were not concerned with suffering because the attraction was more powerful. However, our lifelong group of friends views this option as unacceptable.

3. Dramaturgical

We choose according to the image that we wish to portray. We become actors for an audience. We can play the role of the person who is in love and chooses a good person to live with even though our actual aim is a good life, that is, a secure and stable life with a partner with a good social position and a significant amount of money.

4. Communicative

The three previous types of choice were instrumental. The communicative choice is made through intersubjective dialogue that attempts to reach an agreement with another person or other people. Communication serves to interpret the thoughts, feelings, and desires that each person makes explicit. It is always based on validity claims rather than power claims. Returning to our example, we believe that we will live with good people who offer us security and stability on the assumption that we are in love, because we think that this is a key choice in life. However, we observe that some people who seek stability and security end up "loving" each other but are not "in love with each other." This greatly concerns us. When we feel attracted to other people who we think will fit with our feelings, we explain to them our views, hopes, and fears, thus entering into a dialogue that will help to share and construct the relationship. This communicative action continues with our friends and the people who we most trust.

By way of reflection: Toward a social and intersubjective love

If love is a historical and institutional human invention, then it is logical to eliminate interpretations of love as an instinct or "chemistry." Still, when we do not know the reasons behind a phenomenon, we tend to attribute it to seemingly magical or supernatural causes. In reality, it is quite convenient for us to justify our acts as "inevitable."

The element of "instinct" or "chemistry" is often found in scientific texts and literature on love. Sociological, psychological, and anthropological explanations lead us toward the type of attraction that describes love as an unavoidable lightning strike. At the same time, this type of attraction prioritizes psychological impacts (mostly psychoanalytical) and also poses biology as a deciding factor. Such explanations even link passion to necessary suffering.

Based on Elster (2000), a person can be in love and lucidly control his or her behavior in such a way that negates the concept of a "spontaneous" phenomenon. People do not need to subconsciously search for fathers and mothers in their lovers or want to propagate the human species. If there is no universal law of human nature that inversely associates passion with reason (Elster, 2000: 158), then we can avoid "falling" irretrievably into the arms of the conquering person.

We often fall in love with those who are considered to be good-looking by society and those who represent strength (in each context), that is, with those who have more power than others. This is inextricably complemented by stability and/or security. Attraction and stability, however, can be considered two exclusionary assumptions. By internalizing kindness as synonymous with stability and tenderness, we may separate it from passion and view good people as boring. At the same time, when attraction is considered as synonymous with madness and instability and therefore with passion, we may view people with a "strong character," such as aggressive or violent people, as attractive.

Due to the lack of depth in the current literature regarding the reasons underlying attraction, those aspects that are attractive to men and those that are attractive to women are not considered separately, and the reasons for this are not analyzed. In the same vein, there is a tendency to state that people's values become more important over time, as if values were not part of the initial attraction (or initial lack of attraction). My view differs: attitudes and values are clear from the outset, so it is essential to incorporate them at the level of attraction. Because people's eyes convey everything, we only need to know how to read other people's eyes (and wish to do so). If we do not do it, we may come to the crossroads predicted by Beck and Beck-Gernsheim (1995), who questioned whether it is possible to experience love between equals or whether two parallel lives will never meet.

The last point refers to changes in tastes, desires, and excitement and making a good choice. If we understand why certain types of people attract us, we can alter our socialization through dialogue, debates, and communication. In this way, the internalization process can take place.

The following five ways to carry out choice have been presented: (1) teleological or rational, (2) normative, (3) dramaturgical, (4) emotional or "irrational," and (5) communicative or intersubjective. People's view of attractiveness widely varies: Some people may think that someone is ugly, but other people would say that person is good-looking. We cannot convince everyone of the validity of our judgment, nor do we need to do so. As previously noted (Habermas, 1987a), it is not necessary to reach a consensus on aesthetics (standards of value). However, a lack of knowledge about why we fall in love with a person (truth claims) has terrible consequences, the same as those caused by the fact that there are conquerors who humiliate their victims (rightness claims).

Is it not awful that we fall in love with people who humiliate us? Is it not terrible to ignore the mechanisms of attraction? In this case, Habermas (1987a, 1987b) delved deeper into intersubjectivity (communicative rationality) than did Elster (1999) but did not address the irrationality of emotions in depth. Thus, I described the five types of choice and chose the communicative choice that involves egalitarian dialogue while stressing the management of emotions.

In fact, people do not always make a certain type of choice or act in the same manner. However, choice is crucial when we have not solved the problem of attraction in positive ways: When the wrong people attract us, the first step is to not choose them, and the second one is to modify our tastes, desires, and preferences through engaging in communicative action and process.

· 2 ·

CONTEMPORARY LOVE THEORIES

Elements of Change

"The Risk Society can also put a learning process into place (...) as a global learning process, such as cosmopolitization: and this is essentially, the hope with which I propose my theory (...) May my enemies take charge of killing these hopes. Meanwhile, I continue in search of my objective, which is marvelously unattainable: rethinking society" (Beck, 2002: 195–216).

A large global change is taking place in all of the processes that affect our lives. For instance, the social conflict that was previously evident in social class struggle is now reflected in the battle of genders and in relationships that involve domination. Although questions of love are always similar in their functioning, they are constantly accompanied by risk and uncertainty. Thus, our collective consciousness has incorporated insecurity into the sexual -affective terrain as inherent to our daily lives. These lives take on new forms and open up a pathway toward relationships in which lovers attempt to express their love through dialogue and work to achieve equality and freedom daily.

Contemporary love theories in the social sciences

Does sex speak the language of revolution? Are we experiencing a sexual revolution? What type of connection exists between love and sex? Is it possible to be in a motivating sexual relationship of equals, or are we always dominated by power relations? What has happened to intimacy? Is it being transformed in a subversive way? These are some of the questions that Giddens (1991, 1993) attempted to answer on the topic of sexuality and love. He demonstrated that passion is reduced to the realm of sex in contemporary society because, among other reasons, it does not find a place among the current routine-based schemes that provide us with security.

Giddens's discourse (1993) leads us toward a sexual emancipation that involves sexual democracy. It also warns us that we are progressing through relationships of freedom and equality – based on autonomy – that steal motivation and that we separate exciting sex from boring democracy. However, Giddens did not delve deeper into the topic, confirming that modern sexuality is the embodiment of the failure of a civilization that is dedicated to economic growth and technical control.

Yet Giddens attempted to complete a difficult study in which the subject became a positive agent for social transformation, intimacy was defended as sexual democracy, and stability and passion were seen as incompatible. He also provided refreshing criticism of the systemic world of Luhmann (1986) as well as of the postmodern perspective (Foucault, 1994, 1999; Lyotard, 1987) and its sources of inspiration (Nietzsche, 1985, 1987), as these authors solely focus on power. Some additional aspects of Giddens's work in the field of love and sexuality are discussed below.

If passionate love is linked to sex, and romantic love is linked to the freedom to choose bonds and affection in which sexuality is present but is not the dominating influence, only romantic passion can overcome the current impasse – that seems to have no exit – in *The Normal Chaos of Love* (Beck and Beck-Gernsheim, 1995). The historical solution to the tension between romantic love and passionate love is clearly expressed by Giddens: "The tensions between romantic love and 'amour passion' were dealt with by separating the comfort of the domestic environment from the sexuality of the mistress or the whore. Male cynicism towards romantic love was readily bolstered by this division" (Giddens, 1993: 43). This way of eliminating tension, which is traditionally rooted in male domination (or the recent alleged women's liberation), entails serious social consequences.

Not only does romantic love become incompatible with ardent sexual desire, but its subversive nature (mutual love as the axis of the relationship) also fades as love becomes associated with marriage, children, and lasting "forever." Viewed in this manner, it is not surprising that love has failed as the formula for marriage. Giddens (1993) maintains that at present the ideals of romantic love tend to become fragmented when faced with the pressure of female sexual emancipation that leads to a mutual search for the converging love, defined as a contingent and active love that clashes with concepts of "forever" and "the one and only," which are fundamental in the model of romantic love. Today, divorces and separations are the result of converging love rather than its cause.

Today, in contrast to the ideals of romantic love, love is not monogamous in the sense of sexual exclusivity; even sexuality is negotiated as part of the relationship. Despite this, Giddens (1993) differentiates between more addictive relationships and more intimate relationships typical of converging love. The title *The Transformation of Intimacy* reflects the democratization of daily life as it moves in the direction of emancipation. Among the observed characteristics, the difference between sex in addictive and in intimate relationships is highly revealing. The former links passion with fear and the latter supports sex that stems from friendship and affection.

In contrast to other forms of sexuality, falling in love is intense, exciting, and out of the ordinary (Giddens, 1991). However, it should not lead to an association between passion and addiction, on the one hand, and a pure relationship (Giddens's term) that is linked to sex that stems from friendship, on the other hand. The separation of passion from friendship reflects the most common situation, as desire is sought outside of friendship circles. At the most, we may transform a friend into a partner and experience a progressive loss of passion. In contrast to Giddens, I defend the notion that passion is indissolubly linked to love, including all that such love involves in terms of friendship and affection.

Giddens made such statements as, "However, a relationship today has to be set apart both from what went before and also from the other involvements, sexual or otherwise, which the individuals might have" (Giddens, 1993: 126). It is, however, both risky and ill advised to disregard the other person's previous relationships, the people who he or she was attracted to. When I understand that in the area of love a person is the product of his/her previous relationships, awareness of those relationships and talking about them become an essential requisite of satisfactory sexual-affective relationships.

However, I do agree with Giddens's critique of Foucault: "Sexuality was not created by 'power,' nor is the pervasiveness of sexuality – in any direct way at least – the result of its focal importance for such 'power' (Giddens, 1993: 158). Foucault, who solely focused on power, stated that, "In fact, power produces; it produces reality; it produces domains of objects and rituals of truth. The individual and the knowledge that may be gained of him belong to this production" (Foucault, 1987: 194). Foucault (1987, 1994, 1999) did not identify friendship, love, or solidarity relationships, none of which is created by power. It seems that the nihilistic, fatalistic task of the postmodern perspective involves criticizing and destroying society without providing a better alternative.

Freedom in intimacy implies that we must use the formula "one person, one vote" and ensure the effective participation of all individuals involved to promote debate. If it is true that democracy moves toward the best argument, change must allow for the respect of abilities and help in creating personal bonds. However, one condition is essential – violence must be eliminated. As discussed in the introduction, violence and maltreatment are the result of the relationship model that has developed over centuries. I aim to transform this model. Like Giddens, I believe that reaching freedom in intimacy involves the very persons who set the conditions of their agreement. When transferred into the context of a couple, this involves democratizing intimacy and exposing it to constant negotiation.

On the other hand, Luhmann (1986) viewed love as a symbolic code or a type of password rather than as a feeling. This code or password leads to the genesis of the corresponding feelings. His systemic analysis can be summarized as the defense of highly abstract sociological theories with a rather complex construction, as this is how the historical material can be expressed. He differentiated the relationship between a system and its environment (the abstract other) from the relationship that the system itself has with individualized systems in the environment (the actual others). He considered this distinction (and difference) the result of evolutionary development and examined love accordingly. Luhmann noted that one can only act in love in such a way that he or she can continue to experience the world of the other; meaning must be found in the world of the other:

> The system collapses (even if the partners remain "together") when this ceases to be the common basis that reproduces the system by giving all information the function of reproducing the system (…) and the unity of this system is the unity of difference, which forms the basis of its information processing. One cannot "found" anything on "difference." There is thus (…) no basis for love (…) Every attempt to "see through" the other person ends up in empty space, in the unity of true and false, of sincere and insincere, a vacuum for which there are no criteria of judgment. Therefore, it is not possible to say everything. Transparency only exists in the relationship of system and

environment, which constitutes the system in the first place. Love and love alone can be such transparency. (Luhmann, 1986: 177–178)

He depicted modern society through two accumulated aspects – increased opportunities for impersonal relationships and the intensification of personal relationships. He also observed the need to achieve personal individuality and the possibility that each person may objectify him- or herself and others according to complexity and typology as differentiated from the social system. The conception of communication and of dialogue as generators of knowledge and meaning moves away from Luhmann's (1996) systemic perspective.

The code's form discovers the principle that is established by the code's unity, above all differences. It provides the guidelines that allow one opportunities for communication and, therefore, the ability to transform these opportunities. Consequently, the points of view on which to base love vary. When love was an ideal, it was necessary to understand the qualities of the object. Once it became a paradox, imagination reigned. Now, because autonomy is the key, importance is placed on the reality of what is loved. Specifically, a person is not loved for his or her beauty; rather, a person is beautiful because he or she is loved.

In Luhmann's analysis of current times, he observed the need to find the perfect companion for intimate relationships and commitment. He focused on the way in which autonomy in intimate relationships has changed the situation, examining how external support decreases and internal tensions increase. Therefore, he questioned whether the cause of the problem is the liberation of the intimate relationships that develop as part of the search for personal conformity. The person, as a mere spectator of his/her own existence, remains neutralized. Thus, Luhmann (1986) makes love as passion a claim of the systems: all hope of finding a space for the person's action is cancelled in the name of the God-system. Perhaps the title suggests other conclusions, but the author does not hold back in his contradiction: is he, perhaps, the only conscious inhabitant during the reign of love?

On the other hand, Beck (Beck, Giddens & Lasch, 1997) viewed reflexivity as related to the unknown or the undesired, that is, what occurs involuntarily as a consequence of the process of modernity. Furthermore, Beck and Beck-Gernsheim (1995) considered love to be an achievement of modernity and viewed emancipation as one of the elements of its identity in the face of the traditional rules of life. What occurs in private and may appear to be personal is a consequence of modernity and the freedom that it generates. In other words, we experience the normal chaos of love.

In the past, the situation was clearer. People expected to get married, have children, and educate these children as part of a marriage with an ethical and legal structure that was independent of the couple's wishes (Beck and Beck-Gernsheim, 1995). Currently, the interests of love, family, and personal freedom directly clash in such a way that each person must act and make decisions in a world in which love is becoming increasingly necessary but, at the same time, impossible. Thus it becomes an empty formula that lovers have to live by. What is seductive and redeeming about love *grows* because it is impossible, making very difficult the union of two persons' liberation and self-responsibility, on the one hand, and market dependence, on the other hand. What was previously done without question now requires a dialogue within the home.

With the loss of traditional identities, contradictions regarding the roles of men and women arise in the core of our private lives as though they are personal faults ("everything will go better with my next partner") rather than social configurations. Thus, we begin to refer to the normal chaos of love, around which our lives revolve. For example, as Beck and Beck-Gernsheim stated: "How can two individuals who want to be or become equals and free discover the common ground on which their love can grow? (...) Perhaps the two parallel lines will eventually meet, in the far distant future. Perhaps not. We shall never know" (Beck & Beck-Gernsheim, 1995: 13).

Beck and Beck-Gernsheim (1995) argued that what appears to be a conflict in loving relationships generally has a social aspect:

1. The pre-established gender roles form the basis of industrialized society and are not solely based on tradition, as industrial society (one stratum of it) depends on the unequal status of men and women. Consequently, equality cannot be achieved in these institutional structures that presuppose inequality.
2. The individualizing dynamics only focus on the person (I am myself and then a man or a woman). On the one hand, it frees one from the traditional gender allocations. On the other hand, it leads toward a life as a couple – without God, religion, state, or class, only the "you" remains.
3. The family is considered the place rather than the cause of the outcomes. The problem lies in not only the developing opportunities but

also the increasing obligation to choose, as making decisions can no longer be avoided.

The shift from the industrial society to the Risk Society is similar to the transition from the traditional to the industrial society. It imbues us with a deep feeling of loss of internal stability, a new "disenchantment" with the world. This results in a greater need to find meaning in our lives, which are full of hope and disappointment and that lead us to growing individualization. In turn, love becomes more difficult than ever. How much space is left for a couple with obligations and life plans of their own? Are open relationships a good option? Is living together or living in separate homes better? In the words of Beck and Beck-Gernsheim: "Is it possible for equals to love each other? Can love survive liberation? Or are love and freedom irreconcilable opposites?" (Beck & Beck-Gernsheim, 1995: 65).

Beyond the roles of men and women, we find utopias. To put these utopias into practice, we must transform the current institutional structures that are based on inequality. In the same way that the class struggle generated the notions of equality and freedom, the battle of the sexes will generate other dreams, other neuroses, other realities: "The battle of the sexes is the central drama of our times" (Beck and Beck-Gernsheim, 1995: 45).

Meanwhile, paradoxes appear when we speak of love for love's sake: the dissolution and idolatry of the couple, the desire for descendants and the drop in birth rates, an increase in divorce and a hunger for idylls, etc. All this confirms that love is the key to the cage of normality, promising pleasure and freedom in the creation of the collective world. However, as we know, in the area of attraction, Beck and Beck-Gernsheim stated that love cannot be perfected, it simply happens and "strikes like lightning or dies" (Beck and Beck-Gernsheim, 1995: 198). I believe that these authors should reflect on this crucial subject more carefully, as love must be developed and does not simply strike us down. In the previous chapter on attraction and choice, I discussed not only the social nature of love but also the danger of attributing it to causes such as instinct, "chemistry," "biology," "magic," or "the inevitable," etc.

Finally, entering the psychological area, Sternberg (1998) analyzed the evolution of the loving relationship throughout time, discussing love and its various elements first. His theory sees love as a triangle in which the three vertices correspond to the three elements of intimacy, passion, and commitment.

Intimacy, in terms of the feelings that foster proximity, the bond and the connection, is the result of intense, frequent, and varied interconnections. These interconnections allow the individual to value the loved person, experience intimate communication with that person, provide and receive emotional support, share everything and have a mutual understanding, feel joy in that person's company and rely on him/her, and encourage and hold the person in high esteem. Nevertheless, noting the risk of a loss of independence, Sternberg advocated a balance between intimacy and autonomy: "The swinging back and forth of the intimacy pendulum provides some of the excitement that keeps many relationships alive" (Sternberg, 1998: 9). Although the excitement revitalizes relationships, I find it necessary to object to this in the same way that I must object to the revitalization of relationships through the excitement that violence produces ("after throwing things at each other, we had the best sex ever"), as the consequences are serious and far-reaching.

According to Sternberg, passion, which implies desires and needs that are manifested through psychological and physiological excitement, is developed through the psychological mechanism of "intermittent reinforcement," which is more intense at the beginning of a relationship. He further stated that

> The stimulus that rekindles the passion is similar to the stimulus of the past (…) the pattern of intermittent reinforcement start[s] again, except that this time one has some hope of getting the object of desire. However, if the getting or the keeping is too easy, and continuous reinforcement replaces the intermittent kind, the man may, ironically, lose interest in what he has been seeking. The same principles apply for women, but with respect to the father. (Sternberg, 1998: 11)

In this case, the passion component is closely linked to the behaviorism of reinforcement and psychoanalysis and the frustrated desires are connected to the mother and father. If we compare the stimulus of loving passion to infancy and focus on the "intermittent reinforcement," we neglect the strength of intersubjectivity and the fact that loving passion is an emotion that we can redirect. An understanding that love is social and, therefore, can be transformed through interactions is fundamental. However, the effects of linking love to biological or psychological causes can appear without our thoroughly examining them or searching for a way to transform them by focusing on their social causes and the strength of the communication processes.

Commitment, Sternberg's final element, involves the decision to love a person and maintain this love. Sternberg claimed that commitment saves a relationship during difficult times and fosters the recovery of positive moments, stating, "in ignoring it or separating it from love, you may be missing exactly that component of a loving relationship that enables you to get through the hard times as well as the easy ones" (Sternberg, 1998: 12). Giddens supported this claim by noting that "for a relationship to stand a chance of lasting, then commitment is necessary" (Giddens, 1993: 127).

I believe that commitment should be replaced with intersubjectivity. Through intersubjectivity, intimacy (friendship, stability), and passion (desire, excitement), one will be able to manage the future of relationships. A decision and/or commitment should be replaced with a freely agreed-to consensus based on the best arguments. Based on the idea of intersubjectivity, feelings and the reasons that led to the union must be addressed daily. However, if those two elements disappear, then there is no reason to continue the relationship.

In combining the three elements, Sternberg developed the seven types of love. Of these types, consummate love stands out, as it reflects the combination of the three elements. But it is curious that romantic love (represented by intimacy and passion), "fails" (due to reasons such as distance) because it does not include commitment. In other words, it seems that when people see each other more often, they experience greater love and desire for each other. We must ask if it is really true that couples that spend all of their time together are the happiest and most passionate couples. Does commitment overcome differences when they become insurmountable? Can the effects of distance be decreased through intimacy and passion?

Sternberg focused the evolution of intimacy on certain contemporary theories of emotion in loving relationships (Berscheid, 1983; Mandler, 1980). According to these theories, emotion is only experienced if the common and well-worn interactions are interrupted, which occurs more often at the beginning of a relationship. Then, the frequency of the interruptions and the emotion decreases. Thus, to increase intimacy, a change in behavior is recommended. At this point, we recall Elster's (1999) theory of emotions and the emphasis on stopping the processes of routine and demotivating behavior. Sternberg grounded the evolution of passion on the opponent-process theory of acquired motivation (Solomon, 1980). That is, a relationship begins with a strong positive force that quickly gives way to a negative force that objects to passionate feelings and "balances" the person.

My questions concerning these claims are as follows: What are these negative and positive forces, and where do they come from? Is passion unstoppable or biological, or can it be controlled through intersubjectivity? Is passion controlled by positive and negative natural forces, such as Freud's Eros and Thanatos? It appears as though Sternberg invented negative forces to balance unrestrained passion.

Overall, Sternberg's empirical work is remarkable. He measured love based on his triangular theory using a scale that contains information on the three components. He hoped to inform (heterosexual) couples of the real state of their intimate relationship and thus improve it. Although his theory reminds us of the tests that are available in many magazines and the weakness of their conclusions, his theoretical background and attempt to validate both his triangular theory and his scale should be recognized.

Sternberg also analyzed the significance of the evolutionary theory and its placement of love within a wider biological framework. However, he did not criticize its inability to respond to current revolutionary changes or the lack of alternatives when faced with the alleged inevitability of falling in love, forgetting that intersubjectivity can overcome the great strength of social conditioning factors.

Those who defend the evolutionary theory believe that our childhood influences our future affective relationships, giving them a certain inevitable nature and creating people who are "secure," "aloof," or "anxious-ambivalent." From his investigations, Sternberg (1998) drew the idea that children begin to develop forms of organization at an early age, and these converge into a mixture of the following three types of mental self-government: *legislative* individuals (creators, planners), *executive* individuals (implementers of solutions), and *judicial* individuals (who evaluate people and what they do). These three styles influence future interpersonal relationships. Biological and psychological questions and the social construction of love take on a determining role, and social influence takes on a certain behaviorist tone.

Sternberg also attempted to divert the theory toward power in other ways. He did not emphasize the historical difference between the attraction that power holds in the case of men and the physical beauty that holds in the case of women, a conclusion that fits with the research results in this area. Sternberg stated that we construct love according to the significance that we give it. Although he analyzed and compared various situations with the meaning that they generated, he did not consider intersubjectivity to be the key to relationships and, therefore, to love. Consequently, he neglected the necessary foundations for the creation of meaning, for imbuing life with meaning through interactions, and the communication established in intersubjectivity.

Key elements for tackling love

After examining contemporary theories of love, we developed four key elements that can aid in future investigations of love as follows.

The radicalization of democracy

Emancipation and utopia are two key words in current social theories that have overcome the philosophy of conscience (Searle and Soler, 2004) through communicative action. The authors of such theories include Beck (1998a, 1998b), Beck and Beck-Gernsheim (1995), Giddens (1986, 1991, 1993), and Habermas (1987a, 1987b).

Love is not associated with instinct or solely limited to the conscience. It expands its horizons to intersubjectivity, ensuring that freedom and dreams share dialogues. It demonstrates that what occurs in private and seems to be personal is a direct consequence of societal changes. In examining the transformation of structural forms and analyzing the theoretical-social aspect of love and interpersonal relationships, Beck and Beck-Gernsheim (1995) note that things are not that obvious anymore: Should I get married or live with a partner? Will I have children inside or outside of marriage? Will I live alone, with friends, or with a partner? Currently, a variety of life options are becoming part of an overall curriculum that each person creates throughout his or her life.

Love is justified emotionally and individually rather than traditionally or formally. It is based on the trust, experience, and hope of individuals rather than on a higher entity. Only those who love each other have the truth of their love and the right to it, involving a responsibility even when this love dies out. We delve deeper into the guidelines that Beck established to demonstrate that personal crises and experiences have another side to them regarding the dynamics of freedom that modernity has created.

In the industrial society, patriarchy solved some issues in a simple but unfair manner based on role allocation. In contrast, in the Risk Society, dialogue rules. This evolution allows us to overcome power relations and allow dialogic relations and communication to change the model of attraction that has become entrenched in our intimate relationships.

Beck (1997, 2002), Beck and Beck-Gernsheim (1995), Elster (2000), Flecha, Gómez and Puigvert (2003), Giddens (1990, 1991, 1993), and Habermas (1987a, 1987b, 1989), among others, stated that modernity has not yet exhausted its utopian and emancipatory energy.

Indeed, only the utopian aspect of Traditional Modernity has come to an end, reminding us of the need to radicalize modernity to fit today's society and make real the utopia of Dialogic Modernity (Flecha, Gómez, & Puigvert, 2003). The door to such radicalization is open; we must "make the path by walking."

The protagonism of social actors

Transformations are carried out by actors. The subject has not died, as the postmodern perspective claims. Furthermore, the subject has not been chained to the system, as the systemic theory intends. On the one hand, civic groups have taken the initiative and placed issues that are related to the threatened world onto the agenda. They have accomplished this in spite of the resistance from political parties, the established sciences, and the strength of industry's million-dollar investments. On the other hand, the subject is the indisputable protagonist in his or her love life. This is the case even though the subject displays certain types of behaviors that indicate the clear social influence in the personal domain, an issue that I examine (and harshly criticize) in the discussion of the traditional model of relationships.

Emotions are addressed by carefully examining the role of the person and her world and how decisions can be made in a serene and rational manner (Elster, 2000, 2001). Likewise, the concepts of the lifeworld (Habermas, 1987a, 1987b) and human agency (Giddens, 1986) are utilized when the occurrences of daily life (the chaos of relationships between genders) are viewed as a form of personal enlightenment (Beck and Beck-Gernsheim, 1995). From this perspective, the subject is simultaneously the product of traditions and the initiator of action. Thus, these theories aid in overcoming the determinism of structuralism and functionalism, whose main limitation is that they cannot explain change.

We are faced with two fields of action – one is communicatively constructed and the other is formally organized. Thus, socialization processes are experienced under different conditions and exposed to different risks. The significant changes in the current society are linked to the idea that structures of communication, which have become liberated within families, represent increasingly demanding and, at the same time, vulnerable conditions of socialization. Our choices are multiplied, and our margins of freedom are extended. However, we must make more decisions while avoiding alternatives that can accentuate our insecurities.

Along the same lines, Beck (1997, 1998a) and Beck and Beck-Gernsheim (1995) noted that the individualized lifeworlds almost involuntarily move into a seeking stage. This involves the freedom to express previously repressed impulses and desires based on the freedom to enjoy life in the present rather than the remote future. This also involves consciously developing a culture of pleasure, transforming one's needs into rights, and, if necessary, implementing them against institutional rules.

Beck and Beck-Gernsheim (1995) intuit the danger of passion when they state that all that is delicious, seductive, and the savior of love grows along with its impossibility and acknowledge that what was previously done without asking now requires increasing *dialogue*. I see the contradiction of love as pleasure, trust, and affection and as boredom, habit, solitude, and desperation. After men and women waited many years to become free and equal and thus to enjoy real love (because love and inequality are mutually exclusive), another question arises: Is love between equals possible, or does it lead to the bureaucratization of love?

However, the choice of a partner is no longer subject to outside powers and influences. Therefore, it is easier to maintain a union based on free choice and dialogue. Every day couples move away from the traditional limits of the social environment and the "normal" patterns of marriage. The strength and regulations of the system are recognized. However, we also recognize the protagonist as the person who rewrites her life story through continuous dialogue and communication in search of a satisfactory loving relationship.

The central role of dialogue and consensus

Although we certainly criticize the analysis of the causes of "impossible love" and the potential solutions, we do not apply the same criticism to the social line followed by Beck (1997, 1998a, 1998b, 2000, 2002), Beck and Beck-Gernsheim (1995), and Giddens (1986, 1990, 1991, 1993). Through democracy in intimacy and dialogue, these authors defend and develop people's transformative actions toward a direct and clear evolution that moves away from institutional positions and is grounded on effective communication.

This position is reflected in Beck and Beck-Gernsheim's (1995) definition of this change as something that which was previously carried out without negotiation that must now be discussed and agreements must be reached. This process of change can be broken up and rebuilt, becoming a discursive process. This discourse establishes a type of democracy in love that is not subject to government declarations, legislation, debates, or polls in parliament. Beck states that

> what family, marriage, parenthood, sexuality or love mean, what they should or could be; rather,... vary in substance, exceptions, norms and morality from individual to individual and from relationship to relationship. The answers...must be worked out, negotiated, arranged and justified in all the details of how, what, why or why not. (Beck and Beck-Gernsheim, 1995: 5)

The theorists analyzed here developed a reflexive model, allowing transformation among various groups and social actors. In addition, this model includes an analysis of its own distortions, overcoming the conservative immobility of the structuralist positions of reproduction models and of the post-structuralist positions held by followers of Nietzsche (1985, 1987).

The process of reaching consensus in a couple, family, and other relationships occurs between individuals who may occupy different positions of power. However, this option is better than the imposition of force by the stronger individuals. It also involves the development of dissensus, which can reconstruct later greater egalitarian consensus as part of an intersubjective dynamic that allows people to make democratic decisions about the future transformations and the new spaces.

Giddens linked overcoming violence to a driving force behind the democratization of personal life:

> Violent and abusive relationships are common in the sexual domain and between adults and children. Most such violence derives from men and is directed towards beings weaker than themselves. As an emancipatory ideal of democracy, the prohibition of violence is of basic importance. Coercive influences in relationships, however, obviously can take forms other than physical violence. (Giddens, 1993: 171–172)

Thus, not only does a person become the protagonist in his or her personal relationships, but his or her daily life is also organized according to communicative rationality (Habermas, 1987a, 1987b). Love works through agreements based on arguments that are subject to validity claims. Giddens further discussed a spirit of dialogue and a willingness to reach a consensus, which are fundamental in the *theory of communicative action* (Habermas, 1987a, 1987b): "An individual whose real intentions are hidden from a partner cannot offer the qualities needed for a cooperative definition of the conditions of the relationship" (Giddens, 1993: 172).

If we regulate our actions through communicative processes and subjugate our values to validity claims, loving passion between equals is possible. Otherwise, love and passion do not coincide. In addition, in the current institutional structures, equality between men and women must face obstacles that presuppose gender inequality.

It is possible that this conceptualization of love cannot be fully developed within the capitalist society. This possibility forces us to desperately seek both loving passion and a social pathway that provides an alternative to capitalism. Dialogue and consensus are opening this pathway needed to delve deeper into our relationships and overcome the suffocating systemic perspective.

Meaning and re-enchantment in communication

Beck (1997, 1998a), Giddens (1986, 1990, 1991), and Habermas (1987a, 1987b, 1989) created general theories that seek global explanations of social transformation. Elster (1999, 2000) supplemented them with his theory of emotions.

Habermas (1987a, 1987b) did not attempt to define which values must be agreed upon. Rather, he discussed how to achieve agreement based on understanding between social actors by organizing action-based projects oriented toward social change. The view of love is included within a general analysis based on communicative rationality. Specifically, we no longer use language to achieve a specific aim. Rather, we jointly discover the aim through dialogue, stressing the importance of agreements that are based on equality between the participants in a loving relationship.

In contrast, systemic perspectives have not become oriented toward understanding or social change. Rather, they have served as a vehicle for scientific research through teleological action, being governed by paradigms oriented toward achieving their own power claims.[1] If society overcomes these developments and becomes increasingly involved in the communicative perspective, then it must ensure that the conditions that unite rationality and understanding exist. And it is on that same path of dialogue, of the contribution of arguments and of action by the social actors, that love is setting out its future.

Giddens (1991) claimed that the social circumstances of modernity involve a reformulation of personal identity and individuals because people must adapt to the new life conditions presented to them. People must learn to live without clutching onto the rigid guidelines of the past and impeding adaptation. Furthermore, people must reformulate their identity in their extremely dynamic social context. Hence, loving relationships also undergo significant changes. Transformations in an individual's life represent a reformulation of the guidelines for relationships, in which the loving feeling takes on a new meaning.

Along these lines, Beck and Beck-Gernsheim (1995) discussed the new meaning of love in current society. They argued with Weber's description of the spirit of capitalism as the consequence of early Protestant ethics and stated that in today's context, love is the meaning of the Risk Society. Today, people place their enchantment (meaning) in romantic relationships, the nonmarket, and the search for consolation following the disenchantment of a failed relationship at the same time that they celebrate the liberation of the modern anarchism of love that struggles for happiness before, during, and after the union.

Authentic loving re-enchantment includes mutual finding oneself and mutual self-liberation in a permanent adventure that involves full trust in one's partner. Now that the traditional patterns of love are abandoned and the person *must* choose and make decisions, there are no longer any truths, morals, laws, political parties, syndicates, or parliaments that support the weight of history. The meaning of love changes, marking the transformation from one society to another. Whereas the industrial society stabilized a relationship that was supposed to last a lifetime, the Risk Society leans toward a relationship that is only maintained under specific conditions and seeks the ideal of romantic love, assuming that the relationship will only exist while the feelings last.

Just as Elster (1999, 2000) warned us of the danger of allowing ourselves to be dragged along by emotions, Beck and Beck-Gernsheim refer to hope and action and, simultaneously, to conflict and paradoxes.

> While psychologists usually claim they can best explain all the turbulent relationships by looking at the individuals and how they grew up, and sociologists tend to seek the reasons in external factors like job opportunities and women's rights, we believe the roots lie somewhere else. One fundamental cause of so much emotional upheaval is the inherent contradictoriness of a form of living erected on rapidly changing feelings and the hopes of both partners that they can "become themselves." (Beck and Beck-Gernsheim, 1995: 171)

Relationships have a double dose of tension in the Risk Society. On the one hand, the metaphorical rope pulls us tightly toward the need to be independent. But, on the other hand, it pulls us toward coexistence with other people. This generates tension. However, one must be optimistic and believe that despite the loss of meaning in terms of marriage and families and the growing number of divorces, one can find new meaning through the freedom to unite hearts in a different manner that is better and more beautiful and that fulfills that which has not been fulfilled previously.

By way of reflection: Toward a Dialogic modernity

Today, we begin sexual-affective relationships in a society in which the move toward horizontal relationships and a search for new identities have resulted in a move toward individualization that forces us to create our own life stories from the start. For the first time in history, we are provided with both great opportunities to choose and the obligation to make decisions. This affects our relationships and the guidelines that we must use to take advantage of the opportunities offered by the new social structure. Will we find ways to achieve our dreams? Will a dialogic modernity lead to new utopias?

In the current Risk Society (Beck, 1998a), we must create new ways of reaching consensus, as the old model of instrumental rationality (experts who know about love and laypeople who do not) is no longer useful. We must combine the three spheres (ethics, science, and aesthetics) established by Plato and maintained until the democratic revolutions in such a way that we can overcome both (1) the irrationality of the postmodern perspective, which denies science and morality and places love in the hands of power, and (2) the systemic perspective, which attempts to invalidate our agency.

1. Rebellions against modernity reached their zenith in the postmodern perspective which denies science and ethics in favor of an aesthetic narrative. Reflexive modernization (Beck, 1997, 1998a) and communicative action (Habermas, 1987a, 1987b) demonstrate that modernity contains sufficient strength to forsake the disappointing practice that it generated. A great deal more can be done before we are in danger of falling into destructive postmodern criticism, which states that love is created by power.

2. On the other hand, the systemic perspective allows a double criticism. First, although it examines life as a result of world systems (Parsons, 1951, 1960, 1966), it does not explain why actions in the area of love are often contrary to the criteria of the rational choice theory. Thus,

the system cannot function in these cases. Second, it is equally danger-ous to believe that human agency is the sole generator of transforma-tion and that the system (Luhmann, 1996) absorbs all human expres-sion, eliminating personhood and causing love to occur only between two systems (Luhmann, 1986).

Habermas's (1987a, 1987b) theory of communicative action is compatible with the Risk Society, even as part of what Beck analyzes as the inevitable (not casual or desired) (1997). Habermas indeed sees within the present discourse the potential to rethink the modern one (Habermas, 1989). This optimistic perspective allows us to organize ourselves while encouraging the creation of interconnected networks as an alternative to experts and institutions that are devoid of meaning and incapable of expressing one of the greatest human aspirations – realizing the dream of romantic passion.

Democratization in the public domain is moving toward democratization in the personal domain (Giddens, 1993). We must reconsider the condi-tions in personal relationships, including sex, passion, stability, affection, and equality. Otherwise, democracy alone will not be sufficient. Autonomy does not guarantee romantic passion, not even to consolidate love between people who are equal and free. To achieve this, it is necessary to carry out a continu-ous and in-depth social analysis of what people consider to be personal issues. Otherwise, we run the risk of something which Giddens (1993) himself fears – that democracy may be boring whereas sex should be exciting.

It is clear that we must attempt to free ourselves from structure by rede-fining it, reinventing society and policies, and decolonizing the lifeworld, whose systems tend to colonize. This is an area in which political parties and syndicates, national rights, and frontiers are losing their foundations. Furthermore, the structure of the nuclear family and self-esteem from former types of society are losing not only their foundations but also their legiti-macy. Whereas Luhmann (1986) only considered the absolute power of sys-tems (love can only exist between systems) and Sternberg (1998) sought a compromise that safeguards passion and intimacy, Beck and Beck-Gernsheim (1995) found that communication and dialogue make participation and the transformation of love possible.

In short, this dialogic modernity opens its doors to optimistic love based on the four key concepts that we have developed: (1) the radicaliza-tion of modernity, which shows that love is a quest that aims to overcome the obsolete institutions of the industrial society through the full use of communicative strength; (2) the protagonist's role that we recover through individualization, causing us to rewrite our own life stories; (3) the role of dialogue and consensus in which communicative rationality replaces instrumental rationality, thus allowing egalitarian dialogue that aims for a consensus to achieve profound thought; and (4) the re-encounter with emotions and feelings through a type of communication that seeks new types of relationships and the enchantment of the freedom to choose, all through dialogue and, even, arguments.

With these four key concepts, love is "establishing" its future. We aim in this book to determine whether these key concepts are being practiced and the degree to which they influence people's actions. I examine these topics in Chapter 4, which contains the actual voices of young people. At the moment, the radicalization of democracy, such as the participatory budget for Porto Alegre (Monereo and Riera, 2001); solidarity in terms of promoting progressive social globalization (Sen, 1999), such as the World Social Forum; and feminist movements in favor of the equality of men and women (Puigvert, 1994) as well as critical educational projects disseminated across the Internet are some of civil society's positive responses to the new social structure. I must now elaborate other responses – in the form of models – to the challenges that the processes of attraction and choice represent for all people.

· 3 ·

TWO SEXUAL-AFFECTIVE RELATIONSHIP MODELS

Traditional and Alternative

Taking the above-mentioned contexts and theories into consideration, I analyze the two sexual-affective relationship models that serve as references for my research. Although based on actual behavior, these models are theoretical "ideal" creations that aim to bring us closer to two opposing models of behavior. Therefore, my analysis does not examine whether the models are followed, it only aims to determine whether society is moving closer to them and which of their characteristics are most evident.

One model is historical and quite common. I criticize this model's foundations due to its values and consequences. By contrast, we defend the other model on the basis of its foundation due to its resulting values and effects. Whereas the historical model is based on values from the past, the second model seeks a better future based on the new values of an emerging society. Whereas the historical model is fed by traditional teaching and mixed schools, the new model promotes learning based on egalitarian dialogue and coeducation[1]. Whereas the traditional model reflects the characteristics of a hierarchical social and educational model that separates the different educational agents, the alternative model is framed in a horizontal egalitarian model that combines the efforts of all educational agents in the search for a shared objective.

In short, I examine the traditional model, which defends the notion of attraction as unavoidable passion and places it in opposition to a reasonable and affectionate friendship, tenderness, and stability. I also examine an alternative model that not only defends the idea of attraction as involving passion, friendship, excitement, and stability but also makes a point of selecting tastes, preferences, desires, and attraction rather than viewing them as inevitable. In sum, I examine the values of attraction and choice in both the traditional and the alternative models. I must resolve the extremely important issue of whether the people we choose to share sexual-affective relationships with employ the traditional model or the alternative model.

The traditional model of sexual-affective attraction and choice

This is the classic model, which is considered to be normal when desiring and/or experiencing sexual-affective relationships. Who attracts us and who we choose, in what way, and why are unsettling questions that we examine over the long history of the traditional model. These are ancient questions which often only provoke more questions: "Don Juan is not the man who makes love to women, but the man who women make love to (…) It is a fact that there are men who women fall in love with great intensity and frequency (…) What does this strange talent consist of? What vital mystery is hidden behind this privilege?" (Ortega y Gasset, 1999: 83).

The social basis

The social basis of the traditional model includes certain characteristics that are more typical of earlier societies. It is based on theories of attraction that respond to ancestral patterns and are supported by the instrumental theories of choice. A distant referent is the traditional school, whereas a more recent referent is the mixed school with educational approaches concerning gender equality and multiculturalism. Finally, the sexual-affective objectives and values of this model are those of a society that is hierarchical, authoritarian, discriminatory, and individualistic.

Characteristics of the social context

The model has a clearly vertical nature that reflects social class and patriarchy. Roles are established in such a way that early in life, people know the role that they will play given their social class and gender. A man's role is the head of the family who has a specific profession or career, whereas a woman gets married and becomes a housewife. Traditional society has coexisted with behaviorism (Skinner, 1953, 1974) and has witnessed the struggle for public democracy but not for private democracy, in which certain choices could not be made.

In these societies, white Western males have been prioritized and therefore sexism and racism have been promoted. This prioritization has shaped certain cultural patterns which are transmitted through the cultural subsystem (Parsons, 1951) and has provided social content and social cohesion. These patterns have mainly been transmitted through the family and the school, typical institutions of control and protection. A large number of scholars have discussed the characteristics of these societies. Authors such as Durkheim, Weber, and Marx are undeniable points of reference in the social sciences. In this book, I underline the fact that the traditional model was created in societies that were changing from extended families to nuclear families, moving from the country to the city, from agriculture to factories, and from the community to associations and thus were experiencing anomie (Durkheim), alienation (Marx), and loss of meaning (Weber). In this process, this type of society maintained and adapted patriarchy by allocating roles in an unfair manner as well as categories of experts, social classes or layers; instrumental rationality; the systemic perspective; power relations; and the family institution, political parties, and syndicates; and national frontiers.

The family, education, and development of personality are all viewed in accordance with a previously defined socialization process, in which no action is agreed upon through consensus outside of institutions because everyone is influenced by the economic and administrative system (Castells, 1998a). Thus, communication structures are trapped within formally organized spheres of action and use institutional rules both to impede freedom to express and enjoy as well as to support the influence and power held by others, thus constituting the traditional limits of the social context. There are no negotiations because all is taken for granted (marriage, paternity, sexuality), and the "law of the strongest" is imposed and reflected in institutional structures in which class and gender inequality prevails, diminishing opportunities to choose and make decisions, thus reducing the margins of freedom. This historical period was governed by paradigms oriented toward the success of one's own power claims (Habermas, 1987a, 1987b). In short, there was little space for a more radical democracy that allows the person to be the protagonist in her/his own life story by participating in dialogue and consensus in search of a life full of meaning.

The traditional model is sexist (Espin, 1993; Espin et al., 1996; Subirats, 1997, 1998) and overpowers the feminism of equality and the feminism of difference in any confrontation (Butler, 1999; Nicholson, 1997). This model is not only sexist but also racist: it promotes segregation (Bartolomé, 1997).

Theories on attraction and choice

The traditional model has its most well-established and explicit expression in male symbolism (a spear and a shield showing strength and power) and female symbolism (the mirror of beauty). In this model, the basis of attraction and choice is a socialization process (Berger and Luckmann, 1968) in which the family, school, media, and peer group attach desire, attraction, and excitement to the hero who can cope with all difficulties, including the use of violence, and to the attractive woman who dazzles people with her beauty and submits to the seductive power of the hero. Many examples of this have been shown and continue to be shown in films and gossip magazines.

The family, school and peer group do also link desire, attraction, and excitement with such an almighty hero who can use violence. However, these hubs of socialization (especially the first two) commonly promote affection, friendship, and stability in relation to "good" people who are not viewed as "charming" or attractive. When passion, excitement, tastes, and desires are separated from stability, friendship, affection, and tenderness, the result is unhappiness.

There are two problems with this type of socialization, as follows: (1) feelings of attraction are transmitted to those who have the most power (men) and are the most beautiful (women) independently of these individuals' values and often in spite of their values; (2) feelings of friendship, affection, tenderness, and stability are transmitted to those who do not represent power (boys) or beauty (girls) but who possess good values. Because they are separated rather than linked, a great incompatibility is created between groups (1) and (2). Specifically, the people who are desired, those who excite and arouse great passion, tend to have negative values and do not coincide with those who have good values and transmit stability, friendship, and affection. In other words, (1) represents passionate love that is blind, does not listen to reason, and can end in tragedy, and (2) represents the love that is most advisable when one's goal is stability, although passion is deliberately relinquished.

Entering into the realm of psychology, the traditional model gathers elements from various theories of attraction (Sternberg, 1998), such as the reactance theory (wanting what is difficult to achieve). According to this theory, we desire people who are difficult to reach, but once we obtain them, they immediately lose their appeal, and, similarly, if we seek stability but not passionate relationships, we look for people who are like us. Psychoanalysis provides other theories in which love is sublimated sexuality (Freud, 1975), and womanizers blame their behavior on women themselves (on traumatic separation from the mother), which they use as a protective shield (Giddens, 1993).

Finally, determinants of a biological nature are found in the traditional model. Literature overflows with spectacles of unbridled love that is as inevitable as the suffering that it causes. Writers may view the heart as a machine that prefers and disdains and chooses a predetermined orbit as well as a spontaneous and unexpected manifestation of love that is sudden and eternal. Basing love on biology unavoidably leads to the traditional model.

The different types of choice were discussed by Elster (1996, 1999, 2000) and Habermas (1987a, 1987b); four variations are the basis for the traditional model:

1. *Teleological or rational choice.* This involves choosing according to specific purposes and often making cold and selfish decisions, which tend to take the behavior of other people who enter the relationship into account. This applies both to those who desire a relationship that is not passionate but presents opportunities for rewarding stability and to those who hunt appetizing prey that they will scorn once they have secured it.

2. *Normative choice* involves choosing according to social rules and conventions. It includes a wide range of possibilities, which cover the most general rules of society and pressure from groups of close friends. Thus, different people are chosen according to the values of different groups. For example, a standard scenario includes the family's pressure to choose girls and boys who are "good," the peer group's push for a specific choice based on the environment, and the media's promotion of "passionate" love, which may include varying degrees of violence.

3. *Dramaturgical choice.* According to this choice, relationships in both the subjective and the objective world are part of the theater of life. Some feelings are acted out even though the actor may be internally

experiencing quite different emotions The desire to be liked, the image one wishes to transmit, the important feelings that are hidden, and the feelings that are never acknowledged provide substance to the life in which choices are made.

4. *"Irrational" choice.* Emotions in the subjective and objective worlds are the protagonists. This is one of the worst options, as destructive relationships can be chosen in the name of inevitable love. This is the most typical choice made within the traditional passion-seeking model.

Educational philosophy

Traditional schools, which employ a positivist methodology, are driven by the search for an objective reality. Because these schools' strong point is the academic material, which is independent of the students, it leads to the "banking" approach (Freire, 1970), which is difficult to defend nowadays. Consequently, teachers are sought who not only know the subject matter but also know how to teach to achieve the desired ends.

Therefore, this approach does not consider the relationship between cognitive development and the sociocultural environment. It simply analyzes, observes, and describes as an outsider, thus leading to social and educational reproduction of the present conditions(Bourdieu and Passeron, 1970).

From this perspective, relationships are treated as objective social facts, without providing an opportunity for participation in the content and decisions that must be involved in attraction and choice. In addition, because this perspective does not take into account that cognitive development depends on the context, it does not allow us to transform this context, preventing us from making the relationships that we have better. In some ways, this approach views schools as places where inequalities can be observed but not as places where they are produced or can be eliminated (Jencks and Bane, 1976). In short, the reproduction of sexual-affective relationships involves taking the patriarchal approach, which differentiates between the values of boys and girls (favoring those of boys), and facilitates the development of gender education models that focus on an androcentric and additive curriculum (Thompson, 2001, quoted by Espín, 2002a). Such schools promote sexist stereotypes and develop students' abilities depending on the social behavior that is expected of each gender. Thus, these schools discriminate, create prejudices, and favor the promotion of the male gender across various disciplines.

Lack of equal opportunities and reflection on relationships not only prevent respect for sexual freedom but also foster the development of men who expect to exercise power and submissive women, heterosexuality that opposes any other sexual manifestation, and the tacit approval of the double standard. This double standard is found in "making-out relationships" that use and throw away the partner or in longer-lasting relationships that lack passion. We will not elaborate further because this type of school is fading out of existence. We described it briefly in order to underline the extent to which it has always fit into the traditional model of sexual-affective relationships.

Mixed schools, despite the fact they place boys and girls in the same classroom, advocate the traditional model of attraction-choice in sexual-affective relationships, as the identity of the school continues to be impregnated with this model. Although these schools take into account the relationship between cognitive development and the sociocultural environment, they only aim to adapt to that context (rather than transform it). In other words, although these schools represent progress in comparison to traditional schools, they neither transform the context nor aim to change the model of relationships.

With regard to gender, these schools have begun to take the perspective of women into account. In terms of multiculturalism, the mixed school can overcome the assimilatory and compensatory educational model by recognizing the plurality of cultures. However, male teachers continue to be given greater respect, and male students continue to participate in class to a greater extent than girls do. The textbooks and materials used in the classroom provide examples of traditional values and the different roles that boys and girls play. Subjects that are considered nonmasculine become less important (affective relationships, sensitivity, affection), and the school administration displays a clear hierarchy that favors men. Although it may allow a female approach, this often means that all girls have the same opportunity to adapt to male rules, thus seeking the homogenization of values around the traditional male model. In other words, it legitimizes inequalities.

Based on this scenario, in mixed schools, transformative practices that improve sexual-affective relationships are not implemented and are viewed as less important. At the most, these schools have a specific presentation on health education and/or equal opportunities for both sexes. However, this equality still asserts the supremacy of male values.

A traditional relationship typology

Finally, we consider these key questions: How can we recognize this model in practice? Is there any typical behavior that fits with this model? Is it manifested in different typologies?

In other words, we need a guide to recognize the way in which traditional behavior is manifested. People are now demanding democracy in their intimate lives (Giddens, 1993) and wish to construct personal life stories based on freedom and equality (Beck and Beck-Gernsheim, 1995). However, this evolution has not been followed with regard to the basic qualities of the person one should fall in love with. Let us examine the history of this model.

Historically and symbolically, the feminine symbol has always been (and continues to be) the mirror, representing the goddess of beauty (Aphrodite/ Venus). Throughout history, the most desired women have also been the most beautiful. There have been different standards of beauty over the centuries (art often reminds us of this), but beauty has consistently been the criterion that men sought. We add two ideas to this. First, beauty is a necessary but not sufficient condition. Second, as society has changed, other female characteristics have become more important, such as independence and intelligence. However, beauty is still the most important characteristic.

The symbols of men are the spear and the shield of the god of war (Ares/ Mars). Throughout history, the desirable men have represented strength and power. The most valued men in our culture have more power than others in a particular environment. For example, this man may be the best dancer in a nightclub, speaker at a conference, or singer at a rock concert. In all of these cases, it is power that involves a relationship between the superior and inferior, which may first create dislike and, increasingly, even lead to violence and abuse.

Throughout time, this socialization varies only in type. Furthermore, it provides us with the key to determine who attracts us in a personal and intimate manner that seemingly cannot be altered and the reasons behind this attraction. At the same time, the recommended values – people who treat us well, love us, love peace and solidarity, are always available to come to our aid, give rather than receive, etc. – coincide with the values that we want our friends to possess. Who we are attracted to is governed by values that are the opposite of the recommended values – once they have achieved their objective, they look down on us, are selfish, do not love us or treat us well, are never available when we need them, only think of what we can give them, are violent, etc.

This process, which has taken place throughout history, causes us to experience love, on the one hand, and passion, on the other hand. Love is associated with the stable and amicable, whereas passion is linked to the instinctive and impulsive (Beck and Beck-Gernsheim, 1995; Giddens, 1993; Ortega y Gasset, 1999). If we are not able to break away from this dichotomy, it will be difficult to combine love and passion. However, people view this dichotomy as natural. Specifically, a friend (who treats us with equality) does not elicit excitement, but an individual who is inaccessible, has a high social value, and seems more likely to be violent does.

We can now specify how traditional behavior is personified through three significant sociological types in the traditional model: When we speak of males, we use the term "womanizer" as used by Giddens (1993).[2] We then discuss women who try to imitate the male model. In both cases, we take into account the traditional values that govern the model, that is, the historical and current significance of the symbol of the mirror and the spear and the shield. We then take up the subject of stable couples without passion (Beck and Beck-Gernsheim, 1995; Giddens, 1993; Sternberg, 1998).

Womanizers

This first sociological type has often served as an example of the double standard and represents many women's view of an attractive, energetic, or interesting man: "Not only one woman but many women fall in love with the interesting man (…) no women fall in love with the uninteresting man" (Ortega y Gasset, 1999: 45–46). This man frequently makes "mistakes": "Mistakes, in most of the alleged cases, do not exist: the person is what he seemed to be, of course, only that later the consequences of this way of being are suffered, and this is what we call our mistake" (Ortega y Gasset, 1999: 160).

Giddens (1993) is the only major researcher in the contemporary social sciences to address the subject of womanizers. In his analysis, he recognized some of the distinctive characteristics of this figure, for example, this man (1) conquers women only to then leave them and (2) prefers not to be in a relationship, but when he is in a relationship, he becomes involved in it albeit briefly. The problem (Giddens justifies these men here) is that the man (3) suffers from dependence on women and thus (4) he loves them first and then leaves them to immediately search for other women. However, (5) prior to the relationship, codependent women already sense that they will be eventually rejected.

We only agree with Giddens's first characteristic (conquering and abandoning). The other characteristics he identifies are confusing and questionable: Is the behavior of a womanizer an irrational dependency that is impossible to stop? Do womanizers love and care for women, or do they just use them and then spurn them? How is it possible to analyze a womanizer as a lover who initially falls in love but then abandons the loved one immediately? How can Giddens state that a womanizer becomes involved when his only goal is to conquer and boast of never falling in love? It may be more accurate to state that those women expect rejection because they know or sense the behavior of the "attractive" womanizer and understand his true intentions. If this is not the case, why are women capable of anticipating that they will be rejected by the womanizer but do not anticipate rejection by the "good man"? In short, we believe that it is dangerous and incompatible with the traditional model to claim that the womanizer becomes involved in the relationship and loves women until he abandons them. In the same way, it is not correct to state that such behavior is caused by his dependence on women.

Giddens added a new characteristic to the subordination and humiliation of some women at the hands of certain men: "The impulse to subordinate and humiliate women, such as the previous argument on male sexuality indicates…probably forms part of a generic aspect of male psychology" (Giddens, 1993: 121). Giddens based his claim on the premise that the urges to humiliate and subordinate are characteristic of male psychology. In other words, this would imply that female psychology includes the wish to be humiliated and subordinated. To overcome the problems with this hypothesis, Giddens employed fatalistic arguments. However, his discussions on domination and the concept of the woman as an inferior being clearly refer to a social issue. Although this argument illustrates the consequences of an impulsive psychological type, it leads us to examine the theoretical-social aspect of what we consider to be personal. That is, we refer to behavior that manifests centuries of history.

According to Luhmann (1986), the problem is much more complex. When he examined love as passion, he stated that people have no options because they cannot eternalize the moment. Thus, love for love's sake can exist only in the relationship between systems. This implies the existence of womanizers, of women who imitate the model of masculinity, and of couples who have stability but no passion. From his position, neither the content nor the causes of the traditional model can be transformed, as they are only connections between systems.

Beck (1997) places the emphasis on what is involuntary and unexpected. Beck and Beck-Gernsheim (1995) spoke of love striking like lightning and leaving in the same way, mysteriously. Although these authors analyzed love more thoroughly and accurately than other authors, they found the womanizer to be a given in their discussion. In addressing the so-called "ladies man" (men) or "man-eater" (women), these authors sought an alibi for the typical womanizer model and the female model that imitates it. My response is that love and sexual-affective relationships can be transformed based on the realization that there are no inevitable encounters. Love does not strike like lightning if one understands why it might seem to do so.

Sternberg did not clearly identify the classic womanizer or attempt to criticize this figure. He established the existence of a love triangle (passion, intimacy, and commitment) in which commitment is key and united passion and intimacy because "couples who expect passion to last eternally, or that intimacy remains unchangeable, are predestined to suffer a great disappointment" (Sternberg, 1998: 56). He did not examine the reasons behind attraction and passion more deeply, although he claimed that the duration of both is limited. However, he participated in developing the widespread concept that relates various types of adult behavior to childhood:

> The stimulus that rekindles the passion is similar to the stimulus of the past – the mother. The pattern of intermittent reinforcement start[s] again, except that this time one has some hope of getting the object of desire. However, if the getting or the keeping is too easy, and continuous reinforcement replaces the intermittent kind, the man may, ironically, lose interest in what he has been seeking. The same principles apply for women, but with respect to the father. (Sternberg, 1998: 11)

Here, we note the danger of justifying the behavior of womanizers and of women who imitate that model of masculinity as inevitable and linked to childhood and the family. Such justifications are widespread amongst the authors who are cited in this book: "Family relationships can make children into victims and future executioner because the children follow suit, because the children are the perfect victim, and because in their adult life, they will go in search of their executioner or their victim" (Izquierdo, 2000: 276). Such claims attribute an exclusivity to family relationships that does not correspond to them. As previously explained, faced with behavior that is difficult to understand, any justifications or explanations that seem plausible are employed.

Finally, we incorporate two of the many voices from the world of literature and philosophy. Diane Ackerman (a poet, naturalist, essayist and journalist), is contemporary. The other voice is a great philosopher from the first half of the 20th century, Ortega y Gasset. As Elster (2000) states, when attraction and emotions are caused by complex beliefs, authors in the field of humanities are often informative. However, no profound criticism of this subject [attraction and emotions] can be found within the humanities.

The following describes Ackerman's view of the chemical union of two people:

> when the roller coaster of a crush leads the human being to be brought back down to reality sooner or later (...) The sweet and devastating fever of a crush gives way to drugged peace, to a sense of security and of belonging (...) As women who maintain relationships with married men for years discover, they are not prone to divorce, no matter how much they criticize marriage, no matter how much they promise, and no matter how excited they are about them and how sincerely in love they are with these women. (Ackerman, 1994: 213–214)

The author stated that the fever of a crush is fleeting and that married people who maintain other relationships (it is assumed that these are men) do not end their marriages because they are not prone to divorce. What does not being "prone to divorce" mean? Why is this betrayal not questioned? How can people betray and simultaneously be passionately and sincerely in love? Ackerman utilizes biology to defend the womanizer: "Biologically, it's in the male's best interest to love'em and leave'em. A T-shirt prominently displayed (...) summed up the male imperative perfectly (...) (Jump'em, Pump'em, Dump'em)" (Ackerman, 1994: 166). Although it may sound false, it is quite commonplace to identify passion and sincere love as turning into a cold calculation, in the same way that it is a popular practice to exonerate the Don Juan on biological and/or psychological grounds.

Perhaps the following description of Chateaubriand can shed more light on this issue:

> The woman passes by him and suddenly feels charged with magic electricity. She then gives herself completely. Why? Ah! This is the secret which those who study donjuanism should have revealed to us. Chateaubriand was not a beautiful man. He was small with hunched shoulders. Always in a bad mood, disdainful and distant. His interest in the female lover lasted for eight days. However, the woman who fell in love at twenty, continues at eighty, to be infatuated with the "genius," who she might never have seen again. (Ortega y Gasset, 1999: 85)

This philosopher's appraisal of the womanizer appears to be much more accurate than that of the above authors, although he did not provide solutions (he asked for help from authors in this field), because he believed that this question must be resolved by the natural sciences.

In short, sociology, psychology, philosophy, literature, etc. have not given us a well-developed and clear definition, or an accurate criticism, of the womanizer. In fact, the opposite is true. In these fields, the justifications of the womanizer are psychological or biological in nature or simply left to chance. Oddly, we coexist with womanizers and witness their "exploits" as natural. We may even envy or desire them.

However, my conclusion is quite different. If I consider that reason and passion can coincide (Elster, 2000) and that relationships improve through dialogue, pacts, and arguments (Habermas, 1987a, 1987b), it is clear that the characteristics that womanizers share are in contradiction with Elster and Habermas's hypotheses. Ortega y Gasset (1999) defined womanizers as bad-tempered, disdainful, and distant as well as bearers of a secret that gives them a hold on women that lasts a lifetime. Giddens (1993) wrote that womanizers conquer women in order to then abandon them. Ackerman (1994) claimed that they betray their wives but are not prone to divorce, that their biological instinct leads them to inseminate and move on. Sternberg (1998) justified the male's loss of interest once he has found what he sought.

I conclude that these men conquer and find pleasure in hunting their prey and seek women as a sport. The prey loses her value once she has been conquered (Sternberg, 2000). Contrary to popular belief, womanizers are cold people. As hunters, they calculate their movements in order to trap the prize. In the same vein, in discussing the ethos of romantic love, Giddens (1993) stated that desirable men tend to present themselves as cold and inaccessible. However, he believed that this behavior is going out of fashion because in the new era, "confluent love" leads to equality and reciprocal sexual pleasure, with the cultivation of sexual abilities playing a key role. Giddens linked today's society to the disappearance of womanizers and believed that love-making techniques can resolve relationships.

The maneuvers of womanizers involve calculation and fraudulence. These men are also marked by sadism because they despise their prey following the conquest. Initial gallantry gives way to subsequent derision and indifference. They are incapable of loving or falling in love, and they destroy the hopes and dreams of the women they obtain (Ackerman, 1994). In short, they place their personal technique, coldness, and wisdom into the hands of an evil obsession called "passionate love." Despite having these values (or *because* they have these values), they are capable of generating envy and/or desire.

In other words, the victims of the womanizer, who is most characteristic of the traditional model, are abundant.

The typical choices of this traditional model are specifically put into practice by:

(1) the teleological type (based on purpose), cold hunters who lie in wait for their prey, with variants;

(2) the dramaturgical type (simulating that which he does not feel); and

(3) the "irrational" type, the one who falls prey to the hunter. Yet the force of social norms also plays a role here.

The female version of the womanizer

Feminism has led to great achievements for women, not only in work-related, political, and social fields but also in the area of personal and family relationships. However, there are certain problematic behaviors that require an in-depth examination – for example, the female imitation of the typical womanizer. Giddens noted the existence of these women, although he did not specifically identify them within the model: "Some women – to whom all those things are by now very familiar – might very well opt for a short-term sexual liaison, in the pursuit of transitory excitement or pleasure" (Giddens, 1993: 87). The woman who imitates this model of masculinity contradicts the psychoanalytic explanation of the womanizer's behavior (his dependence on women as a result of his childhood experience of separation from his mother). As previously noted, in the case of women, the problem does not result from the girl's separation from her mother. Rather, it is a social question.

Changes have occurred. As Giddens stated:

> The proportion of women married for more than five years who have had extramarital sexual encounters is today virtually the same as that of men. The double standard still exists, but women are no longer tolerant of the view that, while men need variety and can be expected to engage in extramarital adventures, they should not behave likewise. (Giddens, 1993: 12)

The question is whether such behavior is beneficial or damaging.

In some cases, conquest is a question of planning. In other words, the conquest involves a closed plan that is exhausted once it has been achieved:

> It is enormously attractive, because it is an ingenious game of cunning, which keeps the participants in suspense, feeling welcome and entertained. Its expiry date is

ruthless: once the prey is caught, the hunt is over. This is the project of the Don Juan or the Doña Juana, which has become a myth due to the constant seduction, a brilliant and fun project which, unfortunately, always needs a Doña Inés, whether male or female, to pay the price. A person who is pathetic and fanatical, thinks against all good sense that he or she is an exception and that he or she will manage to transform the Don Juan cynegetic project into a project of love. (Marina, 2002: 166–167)

This passage describes the hunting process and the hopeless idea that the hunted person will transform the affair into a love story. Furthermore, the woman is presented as an executioner rather than a victim. However, the explanation is the attraction in the game. In other words, "We could say that, really, the creative talent is the skillful management of limitations. A poker player's talent implies playing well with the cards he has, which may be not very good cards" (Marina, 2002: 167). The significance and consequences of the Don Juan and Doña Juana figures, who damage their victims, are underestimated. At the same time, the reasons behind their behavior are reduced to a simple and ingenious game of cunning.

However, one of a woman's possible responses to the behavior of the "conquerors" is to retaliate by imitating the model of masculinity. Amongst other things, this behavior involves the following three serious problems:

1. The act of using other people and then "forgetting them" involves destroying hope, not only for those who have good intentions but also for those who are seeking a relationship based on feelings. Womanizers do not fall in love. Thus, who do women retaliate against? Despite this, Giddens, who maintained that womanizers fall in love, ended the sentence about women who seek short and transitory relationships as follows: "For such women, the appeal of the lady-killer fades quickly or is deliberately kept in check" (Giddens, 1993: 87). It is rather difficult to change behavior if we do not accurately recognize and describe the situation.

2. It is frustrating to consider that equality is achieved by imitating a model based on inequality rather than by imposing a different model of behavior and sexuality: "Love and inequality are, after all, as mutually exclusive as fire and water" (Beck and Beck-Gernsheim, 1995: 13). When a woman adapts to the traditional model that dominates our society (in which patriarchy is imposed), she experiences a negative impact, both in the short term and in the long term. Rather, liberation should lead women to believe that "Men's liberation is a passive

affair (…). One probably unintentional result of women's lib is men's lib" (Beck and Beck-Gernsheim, 1995: 152).

3. With the passage of time, male womanizers become more sought after, whereas a woman is considered to be "easy." The injustice of this judgment does not eliminate the consequences of a game that the woman now appears to actively collaborate in.

The different types of choice that are developed as part of this traditional model correspond to those of the womanizer. In other words, the womanizer's choices are teleological, dramaturgical, "irrational," and, at times, normative.

Stable but passionless relationships

The antithesis of womanizers and of women who imitate the model of masculinity is a couple that specifically relinquishes passion in favor of a life with good people, affection, friendship, and stability. The fear of losing everything if they incorporate passion into the relationship makes these couples accept a stable relationship without passion. The same results are obtained when attention is not paid to profound communication processes, allowing the relationship to culminate in greater stability to the detriment of passion. In some cases, a relationship that is based on friendship but has no passion is directly chosen. In other cases, a relationship that began with desire becomes one with friendship but no desire.

In an attempt to justify the effects of socialization, Sternberg (1998) predicted that passion does not last forever and that those who do not believe this will suffer great disappointment. This claim places great importance on commitment, which may save relationships when passion is lost and intimacy is decreased.

As previously mentioned, in an examination of the evolution of loving relationships toward democracy, Giddens (1993) worried that these relationships will revolve around a home that serves as either a headquarters where each person lives their life independently or as the center of a relationship that is based on friendship and affection but lacks passion and desire. He believed that relationships of freedom and equality that are based on autonomy remove motivation and separate exciting sex from boring democracy.

The family and the peer group are likely to applaud the "sensible" decisions made by those who wish to settle (and relinquish their desires) to enjoy a stable home that is solid and secure. We refer to this as the bureaucratization of love. If people oppose a change in values, tastes, and preferences or simply believe that it is not possible to transform them, then this "stable" position is understandable. The fear of falling in love with a person who may later despise you renders the search for passion useless, as it is identified with suffering and a loss of stability.

With regard to choice, the most frequently encountered types are those linked to social norms, although teleological choice is also included in the search for stability and dramaturgical choice involves simulating a passion that is not felt in order to achieve security.

An alternative model of sexual-affective attraction and choice

The success of the alternative model depends on the four keys listed in the conclusion of Chapter 2, as they summarize how to tackle love in the new social context. These keys are the radicalization of democracy, the protagonism of social actors, the fundamental role of dialogue and consensus, and re-enchantment in communication. The future of sexual-affective relationships relies on overcoming the limitations of the traditional model in terms of attraction and choice.

These issues, which always involve risk and uncertainty (Beck, 1997, 1998a; Beck Gernsheim 1998), must use progressive values as a guide, because we are now connecting to a different type of modernity, in which we must create our life stories by choosing between different models and developing new ways of life. We must construct love based on dialogue, equality, and freedom. Furthermore, Giddens (1993) led us toward the type of sexual emancipation that involves sexual democracy. Specifically, the democratization of personal life is a process that has many implications and runs the risk of separating passion from affection and friendship. The alternative model considers this separation quite dangerous. If we create a theory based on a model that involves the type of love that leans toward emancipation, then this love (and the stability and affection that it entails) must be united with passion to retain credibility.

Those who establish new sexual-affective relationships must also take into account knowledge about the other person's previous relationships, that is, what occurred and the sexual and other implications of the occurrences. With regard to this, we attach significance not only to relationships that involve stability but also to sporadic relationships, for example, one-night stands, spontaneous sexual encounters, and so on. Contrary to some authors' beliefs (Giddens, 1993), because one of the essential elements of the alternative model is interaction and communication, this model places key importance on previous relationships. This model also recognizes the importance of having a dialogue about these past relationships to determine their reach and the issues to be modified for the present and the future. What was previously done without asking and involved pre-established roles now requires dialogue and a type of equality between men and women that finds institutional and daily life structures denoting equality essential (Beck and Beck-Gernsheim, 1995).

In short, this new alternative model responds to the Becks by stating that love between equals is possible, love after emancipation exists, and love and freedom are not irreconcilable opposites. In fact, it responds to them using their own words within a different context: "A mere utopia? We can only try" (Beck and Beck-Gernsheim, 1995: 77).

The basis of this model

The model is based on the transformation of traditional theories on attraction through a change in tastes, preferences, desires, excitement, etc., which now responds to new progressive values as the corollary of attraction. It focuses on intersubjective choice and communicative choice (Habermas, 1987a, 1987b), with special attention to emotions (Elster, 1999, 2000). It develops the only choice that is communicative rather than instrumental. It uses the coeducation school as a role model. In addition, it seeks the equality of difference in terms of identity, fights against discrimination, and develops values of solidarity by finding meaning through interaction and communication that is established within it.

Characteristics of the social context

The alternative model is compatible with the characteristics of the new society. The transformation from the agrarian to the industrial era resulted in a change in structures and ways of life. Now, the industrial era has become the information and/or risk era, which has its own structures and lifestyles. Structures are increasingly being transformed through a constant dialogue with the I. Similarly, thoughts and feelings are united in the search for identity and meaning in the network society. This involves ending patriarchy and resolving the battle of the sexes. This may be achieved through communication and dialogue in a context that is more horizontal, flexible, and comprehensive. In contrast to the traditional model, which aims to retain hierarchical relationships, the alternative model must involve such communication and dialogue.

This new type of society, which affects institutions and our ways of life, allows us to construct identities (Castells, 1998a) in search of our own social transformations and that of the entire social structure. We have a great opportunity to become new agents of social transformation by eliminating one traditional conviction – that the man is in charge. This situation must be rectified by love between equals without a reduction in motivation.

However, in this society, risk is in charge (Beck, 1998a; Beck et al., 1997). Risk even takes on the question of love, incorporating insecurity as a typical component of daily life. Therefore, this new model must lean this risk toward solutions that link us to a type of relationship in which love is not only a dream but also a required task based on communication and the daily incorporation of equality and freedom. There are no longer any aspects of love that can be taken for granted.

The alternative model does not revolve around social classes or patriarchy or support pre-established roles. It is based on freer choices, through which all can be negotiated (marriage, parenthood, sexuality, etc.), and the "law of argumentation" is imposed on it. Love is no longer associated with instinct or tied to the philosophy of the subject or of consciousness. Rather, it takes on significance through intersubjectivity and is justified emotionally rather than traditionally or formally. Communicative force must be used to analyze and change the traditional model of attraction in intimate relationships.

This new model is directly opposed to sexism and racism; it does not unfairly allocate roles or promote categories of experts, professions, classes, or economic strata. Its identity lies in communicative rationality, substituting more dialogic relations for power relations. Thus, it defends the feminism of the equality of differences (Puigvert, 2001; Subirats, 1997, 1998). This model involves family, education, and the development of personality in a process of socialization supported by a search for consensus outside of institutions. This is because, in addition to the pressure of the financial and administrative system, we develop areas of action that are communicatively structured and allow us to be protagonists in our own love lives. This increases our opportunities to make choices, the margins of our freedom and our decision-making ability, even by attacking and/or transforming institutional rules in search of a meaningful life.

Theories of attraction and choice

As previously mentioned, passion and reason are not in opposition. As Elster stated: "There is no universal law of human nature which expresses an inverse relationship between passion and reason, although perhaps there could be a statistical negative correlation between them" (Elster, 2000: 158).

The alternative model defends the position that in processes of attraction and choice, we must consider people's values (and, if necessary, reject them). If these values are negative, we should not fall in love with that person. This model rejects statements such as "Everyone knows that love is blind and does not pay attention to reason" and does not consider love to be an instinct, chemistry, or a signal from the heart. Rather, it considers love to be the manifestation of internalized values that indicate who is desirable (the result of social influence).

The dilemma occurs in determining how to address the socialization that impacts motivation or a lack of motivation and how to transform "what is inside us" so that we can have a loving relationship that is both stable and passionate. If socialization occurs based on what we experience rather than what we would like to experience and if the people who we interact with, desire, dream of, and fantasize about have opposing values, then we must engage in reflection and dialogue. This allows us to begin the search for people who we desire and who also share our values.

We must deeply consider why we find certain people and how they attract us (real socialization processes). Furthermore, we must answer such questions as why the same people attract many different people and why attraction tends to be accompanied by subsequent rejection and dependency as well as the roles of the conquerors and the conquered. In our discussion of Sternberg (1998), we examined how to analyze attraction, taking into consideration the difficulty of achieving similarity, complementarity, the sequential filter, the stimulus-value role, the dyadic formation, and practical theories.

When there is only an in-depth analysis of that which (inevitably) attracts but not an analysis of the reasons behind attraction, then psychoanalysis is the favored approach because it attempts to provide a response to this behavior. According to the alternative model, neither psychoanalysis nor research in biology or "chemistry" can explain what only centuries of history can clarify concerning attraction and choice.

In contrast to the traditional model, which draws from the principles of past societies, the alternative model takes into account that everyday opportunities to choose as well as the obligation to do so are being further developed. In that task, it uses communicative or intersubjective choice, which is the only type of choice that is not instrumental. Communicative rationality, as guided by pretensions of truth (science) and rectitude (ethics), allows for a change in tastes, preferences, desires, and excitement. It converts dialogue, debates, interaction, and communication between equals into key concepts that lead us to the resocialization of our guidelines for attraction and choice. This ties in with the progressive values that lead to stability and passion at the same time and with the same person.

Educational philosophy of the alternative model

Only the coeducation approach focuses on the communicative perspective and considers social reality to be a human construction in which meaning is constructed communicatively through interaction. Based on knowledge of the material and the people and groups who are learning, teachers have the opportunity to carry out dialogic learning and address the relevant methodological gap in such a way that they interact in a horizontal manner. Thus, the context and sexual-affective relationships can be transformed. Therefore, when applied to coeducational schools, the communicative perspective generates transformation (Elboj, Puigdellívol, Soler, and Valls, 2002).

Based on this approach, relationships are treated as a product of the interaction and the communication that take place, rather than as objective social facts that do not give people the opportunity to participate in the decisions concerning attraction and choice. In coeducational schools, inequalities are not only observed but also taken into account so they can be changed. We are now facing real equal opportunities to reflect on relationships and respect for sexual freedom and to facilitate healthy affectivity and sexuality.

Logically, coeducation should help us to abandon the traditional model. However, although there is widespread agreement that we should eliminate a disciplinary model that incorporates behaviorism and generates expulsions and punishments as well as truancy and conflict, the administration of coeducational schools tends to prefer the mediation model. Although the mediation model is a clear improvement over the disciplinary model, the problems of professional experts and the reinforcement of stereotypes, among others, arise.

Sexual-affective relationships should be immersed in a community-based educational model that focuses on prevention of incorrect information, real community participation, and interactive groups.

An alternative relationship typology

The traditional model of relationships incorporates three types (womanizers, women who imitate that model of masculinity, and stable but passionless couples). However, in the alternative model, there is only one type – friendship and passion with the same person – although it may be displayed in different forms. Whereas the traditional model types are developed "naturally" in our daily lives, the alternative model involves changing or reprogramming these traditional values to progressively transform attraction, choice, and loving action.

If no action is taken, then people's most intimate emotions will continue to be supported by traditional values that are internalized through socialization processes. These values are slowly incorporated into our own experience and construct the model of attraction which functions as biological or anthropological. Those who have not transformed the model of attraction cannot create the ideal of romantic passion. Thus, they must first utilize the following three potential alternatives:

(1) Choosing people who attract according to one's socialization and traditional inherited values but who are not suited to the chooser. This includes a period of excitement, waiting, tension, and overwhelming happiness (sowing the seeds of hope and passion) but eventually leads to disaster and suffering.

(2) Choosing those who do not attract but possess the recommended values of the society. This involves choosing well but without passion and aspiring to have a deep friendship and love for each other. In other words, the choice is stability with a good person who is not exciting and does not generate fantasies, a relationship in which there is no "glow in people's eyes" and they miss out on "something" that is provided by those who attract but are not recommended.

(3) Not choosing a partner. This option avoids the suffering caused by those who attract but are unsuitable partners and the boredom of

those who do not attract but who provide well-being. This decision is reasonable but not satisfactory because it involves abandoning the possibility of a positive, though sometimes difficult, sexual-affective relationship.

Wee must develop and recognize the alternative model in daily practice. Because the model is not widespread or well known, I need to describe some of its guiding premises.

Guiding principles

1. Good information and communication processes, which forestall the concealment of important emotions and feelings and superficial discussions on sexual-affective issues. Such processes facilitate an in-depth discussion of feelings, sensations, thoughts, desires, etc., thus transforming attraction processes and allowing us to avoid the three traditional model types.

2. Unifying personal and social transformation. This concerns debating and negotiating love not only as a dream but as a task that must be carried out based on communication and the daily establishment of equality and freedom. Progressive social change ties together what has been happening in the educational model and sexual-affective relationships in general.

3. Direct opposition to sexism, racism, the category of "experts," and power relations. The equality of difference and validity claims allows both persons to be protagonists in loving relationships, thus increasing opportunities to choose as well as the margins of freedom and decision making.

4. Rejection of the notion that love is based on the workings of the sciences, biology, or anthropology (instinct, chemistry, or signals from the heart). Instead, one must understand love as a social question that involves the display of the values that have been internalized over many years.

5. Acting on the basis of communicative or intersubjective choice (the only type of choice that is not instrumental), making possible the change in tastes, preferences, desires, and excitement through egalitarian dialogue and discussion. This obliges us to constantly revise our values and what we incorporate into daily events. Furthermore, it involves

engaging in dialogue based on equality and evaluating the significance of having an impact on rules, interests, and, above all, emotions.

6. Coeducation schools allow us to focus on the communicative perspective and the communitarian model. This model emphasizes prevention, real community participation, and interactive groups, thus directly rejecting the disciplinary model and replacing the mediation model.

7. Dialogic action through dialogic learning transforms the context and sexual-affective relationships in the context.

Dialogic action and dialogic learning

The new model defends a process of sexual-affective change that must form part of cultural dialogic action, which finds passion and affection in the same person and thus confirms that equality and passion are not opposing terms. In that process, we all contribute our knowledge and choose the subjects to discuss in a critical way to avoid emotions to overwhelm us. So love does not have a biological and/or chemical basis: it is an emotion that expresses feelings based on learned knowledge.

The concept of dialogic learning and its seven principles are applied to the sexual-affective terrain (Flecha, 1997). Thus, we construct the alternative model of sexual-affective relationships, adjusting to the intersubjectivity that guides this choice through egalitarian dialogue, which, in turn, is governed by the validity of arguments rather than positions of power.

1. **Egalitarian dialogue:** We learn and question the various statements presented without the imposition of knowledge that is culturally hegemonic and establishes the material and learning rhythms of enduring authoritarian and hierarchical relationships. Without such impositions, this dialogue involves convincing and thus thinking and searching for new reasons. At the same time, other people's arguments could lead to the discovery of one's own mistakes. This system would increase learning in our schools, families, and peer groups.

   This horizontality helps to overcome the larger influence of some voices, and everyday contributions are given greater value regardless of people's educational level or gender. Egalitarian dialogue entails debates because there are not only different opinions but also conflictive situations. However, the issue lies in how we resolve these problems. In this particular case, we resolve problems using the best arguments, constructing interpretations, and organizing sexual-affective relationships based on dialogue and consensus without being controlled by "irresistible" personal emotions or the power that people impose on us.

2. **Cultural intelligence:** All people have the same capacity for argumentation. The cultural system assumes that a certain type of academic intelligence will prevail, but love should not be tied to academia. Rather, it should fend for itself in every form of communication. This is because every person and group can overcome the barriers, exclusion, and discrimination in the terrain of love. Based on this perspective, we do not believe that a select minority holds the knowledge that dictates and imposes how, when, and who one should fall in love with. Furthermore, we do not believe that this minority should determine which people or social groups to exclude. On the contrary, we believe that good communication can promote self-confidence and creativity and overcome sexism and racism, thus surmounting the great number of complexes and insecurities that we accumulate in the sexual-affective field.

   This entails a re-evaluation of practical intelligence and communicative abilities. At the same time, we must be open to people from different cultures who can enrich the current relationship situation through their contributions, views, and abilities.

3. **Transformation:** People who uphold the systems theory (all is established in structures which do not allow us to contribute to the book on love) warn that all actions feed the system and that we should not tire ourselves by fighting to change loving relationships because relationships are unavoidably reproduced by the cultural system. Womanizers, women who imitate that model, and stable, passionless couples are constant reminders of the unavoidable reproductive mechanism. People who uphold the subject theory (if we have created the structures, we can also change them when we wish) encourage us to embrace and engage in change. They believe that if we decide to change them, our sexual-affective relationships can be modified at the rate that each person selects.

   The position concerning the dialogic learning of love differs. The person who adopts this position equally believes in systems and subjects and does not conceive of society without the influence and intervention of both. The communication produced through egalitarian dialogue has a great transformational impact, as horizontal relationships transform situations of exclusion into situations of participation. Despite the cultural system, Freire's (1997b) statement that we are beings of transformation rather than adaptation and that animals are the only beings that adapt continues to echo.

Transformation refers to a change in the relationships among family members, among students and teachers in a classroom, and between all of the people in a school and their environment. Progressive social transformation is not possible without the existence of a parallel personal sexual-affective transformation. They are dependent on each other such that they form part of the same process, in which one cannot understand one without the other. For example, we are individuals and society at the same time.

4. **Instrumental dimension:** All of the information provided thus far runs the risk of being reduced to a nice chat over coffee if we do not stress the instrumental aspect. We must know how the social influences the personal, how and why we fall in love, who we fall in love with, what the environmental influences are, how we internalize these influences, and what the operating mechanisms are. Dialogic learning has the necessary skills and knowledge to advance toward the development of a new alternative model of attraction-choice in the sexual-affective terrain based on a scientific knowledge of love that does not view love as a biological, anthropological, or "chemical" emotion. If the history of love is not that of destiny oriented by external forces and cannot be confused with instincts, then the socialization and internalization of tastes, attractions, desires, and preferences are much more social than personal. Therefore, this internalized "chemistry" can be deprogrammed by eliminating the sexual-affective weight of the traditional model and reprogrammed with new values, including friendship and passion at the same time and with the same person.

5. **The creation of meaning:** The sexual-affective field can deeply disappoint us, remove meaning from a large part of our lives, and cause us to concentrate on other subjects so that we may "forget." Dialogic learning is a high-caliber resource that helps to overcome this loss of meaning and, consequently, helps create other meaning in our lives. Dreams and feelings provide meaning to our existence; however, we need egalitarian dialogue to guide ourselves toward the changes that we must make to develop creative abilities and a fuller life. Social and educational contexts are spaces for discussion rather than spaces

for silence. In regards to dreams, a new dilemma arises when affection and passion are sought at the same time, for a long period, and with the same person. In the traditional model of relationships, this connection of affection and passion is not possible because the model separates stability (husband or wife) from passion (lover). In the alternative model, however, this connection is feasible because the values are exempt from the double standard and help to create meaning in our lives. This meaning unites kindness with attraction and violence with rejection.

6. **Solidarity:** If that which we consider to be personal – for example, which people attract us – is a reflection of the social (that is, if the guidelines for the cultural system are transmitted to us in such a way that we internalize them as biological or anthropological), then our response to this socialization cannot be carried out on a personal level. We do not have sufficient knowledge or ability to successfully face these "biological" emotions. Furthermore, we are better able to observe and recognize phenomena when they don't affect us personally. In other words, we need each other's help to advance and create new forms of sexual-affective relationships.

   If a person feels that she is overwhelmed by an irrational and unstoppable emotion, it is difficult to believe that solidarity can have a decisive impact on her sexual-affective life. However, people do exert influence and allow themselves to be influenced. The problem lies in the specific influences and the types of people who guide us in our decisions. If we believe that we are capable of making a poor choice, we can ask people to help us avoid a wrong decision. This does not mean sacrificing freedom or losing autonomy. Rather, we can implement knowledge, dialogue, and joint reflection to avoid relationships that could destroy us. Solidarity leads us, for example, to form heterogeneous interactive groups rather than homogeneous ability groups. In practice, it leads us to value democracy, equality, peace, and sexual freedom rather than dictatorship, inequality, war, and rape.

7. **Equality of difference:** The value that guides dialogic learning in love is equality, which includes respect for difference In a situation of inequality, the culture of difference, which "ignores" equality, reinforces as "different" what is exclusionary and does so through adaptation to difference, which produces greater inequalities. By contrast, the progressive outlook is marked by all people's equal right to experience a

dignified and full sexual-affective life. The right to difference or diversity has been traditionally understood as follows: some people or groups have a right to everything, whereas others do not have a right to anything. Sexual-affective relationships that involve power, violence, and selfishness are included in this right to everything and are defended in the name of each person's freedom to do as he or she wishes. The right to equality has also been understood as people having the same relationships, homogenizing the concept of equality and distancing it from its progressive interpretation. In other cases, this right has been limited to the equal opportunity to have satisfactory relationships. However, because it does not take into account the fact that each person has a different background, some people go far, whereas others remain at the beginning or halfway down the path.

Dialogic learning does not agree with either the homogenizing or the "diverse" position, as it considers all people to be equal and different. Therefore, it promotes the right of every person to live in a different manner while learning what he/she considers to be necessary in his/her sexual-affective life. This position is defined through the dialogic perspective, which seeks the transformation of the environment to achieve better relationships. Along the same lines, Beck and Beck-Gernsheim's (1995) question arises again, although it is reformulated: Is possible for passion to exist in an egalitarian relationship or are equality and passion always opposed to each other. The traditional model has stated that relationships between equals lead to friendship but not to passion or desire. Friendship is sought in the good person, and passion is reserved for those who use and/or mistreat people. In the new model, solidarity, stability, and passion are simultaneously promoted through egalitarian dialogue. This facilitates the transformation of relationships and creates meaning in life. These dialogic and egalitarian practices allow us to construct sexual-affective relationships that are exciting and arouse passion in people who truly love us.

By way of reflection: Toward a new model of relationships

In this chapter, I analyzed the two contrasting models in terms of "ideal types" that characterize sexual-affective relationships. The traditional model embodies the conventional values developed over the course of centuries. This model has been adapted to many societies but has always been based on a conservative and sexist idea that leads to unequal and unsatisfactory relationships. The double standard separates passion, desire, excitement, and irrational behavior from sweetness, stability, friendship, and affection.[3]

I first discussed the classic figure of the male conqueror – cold, inaccessible, calculating, and false and takes pleasure in hunting his prey. The sole aim of his hunt is to obtain the prey. Once the objective is achieved, he grows distant, thus showing his prey that she has lost her value and attractiveness and generating a feeling of insecurity and masochism in her. These feelings are in proportion to the dose of sadism that the conqueror administers after each conquest. He destroys the hopes of the women he obtains by acting out a "passionate love" that he does not feel. The woman who imitates the traditional Don Juan model expects to gain her freedom through this role. The objective continues to be cold, calculating, and sadistic conquest, generating a strong feeling of insecurity in the people who are conquered and then despised. This model has the following three consequences: (1) a false liberation, which leads to dissatisfaction; (2) the hunt for boys who are not womanizers and therefore these women do not manage to take "revenge" on actual womanizers; and (3) a reputation of being "easy." The Don Juans, on the other hand, enhance their reputation and are viewed as "smart."

The third ideal type involves resignation. People desire passion, blindly falling in love without considerations, being crazy in love, and experiencing excitement with no limits. However, the womanizer and his female equivalent demonstrate that passion only leads to ruin. Therefore, it is important to avoid or exit from this slippery terrain. The consequence of this perspective is a search for stable, affectionate, and friendly relationships that are divorced from passion. Being bland and without the ability to charm is linked to being good, friendly, sweet, and egalitarian. This duality, which has been maintained and developed throughout history, has placed passion and friendship, affection and excitement, and stability and desire in opposition. Security and being treated well take precedence over attraction and desire such that responsibility, rationality, a good public image, respect, reflexivity, friendship, and dialogue are prioritized. On the other hand, neither love as passion nor exciting sweetness is considered.

In short, the traditional model, which responds to the historical and social context, defends attraction as synonymous with desire and passion and antonymous with sweetness and stability. This model is based on the notion that attraction is irresistible and impossible to avoid and follows the preferences dictated by our heart. The conquest and the game place weapons in the hands of those who are considered attractive: They hunt, chase, and harass the prey until they obtain it. Finally, the model contains the following counterpoint: relationships that focus on stability, friendship, [and] affection but lack passion.

This model is compatible with traditional schools and modern schools that contain both traditional and some progressive elements, with an educational model based on a hierarchical society and the institutional separation of power within and between institutions (basically, the school and the family). This is done in such a way that they impede both an authentic egalitarian education and programs and curricula in which sexual-affective education plays a predominant crosscutting role and displays certain progressive values.

The alternative model responds to the doors opened by investigating relationships in the new social context. This model is based on a love in which we are the protagonists, writing and rewriting our life stories through dialogue and consensus, and in which communicative rationality allows a depth of thought and feeling that leads to understanding. It defends attraction as synonymous with excitement and affection, as well as with friendship and desire, stability and obsession, and passion and sweetness. It treats tastes, preferences, desires, and attraction as choices rather than "inevitable" events that suddenly emerge from the deepest part of our being. It seeks the weapons of attraction in progressive values and promotes the criterion of intersubjective or communicative choice, particularly with emotions. The question lies in connecting and directing our attraction toward people who have progressive values so that the impulses that are hard to control do not contradict the recommended values.

Therefore, we do not choose people who initially attract us by providing days that are filled with excitement, expectation, and overwhelming happiness but then lead us to misfortune, self-hatred, and suffering. We also do not choose those who do not attract us but have good values because we do not aspire to friendship without passion. We do not choose an individual simply to avoid making a mistake. We do not wish to feed our intimate emotions with the traditional values. These emotions should be based on the alternative values, which transform the model of attraction to make the ideal of romantic passion possible.

The alternative model helps to overcome the long-standing problems of the traditional model. Dissatisfaction in relationships, based either on "flirting" (passion without love) or stability (love without passion), can only be overcome by uniting affection and excitement, friendship and passion, and stability and madness in the same person. Thus, the model incorporates the principles of dialogic action (in which both participants contribute their knowledge, thus transforming affective and sexual reality). It also incorporates the principles of dialogic learning (in which interpretations are constructed and affective relationships are organized based on the best arguments without putting our trust in a select minority to tell us who we should fall in love with, how, and when). The model concerns the creation of dreams and feelings that provide meaning to our existence through egalitarian dialogue, respect for the equality of difference, and solidarity. It also involves good communication (i.e., sharing the most important parts of our emotions and feelings) and making a good choice. If this choice is dictated from "inside," it should involve a change in tastes, preferences, and desires – that is, a change in attraction.

This model fits with coeducational schools and an educational model based on horizontality and the egalitarian participation of the entire community. The model also allows and encourages the development of a curriculum in which critical sexual-affective education becomes essential. The ideal type of school is represented by a model of community participation that contains all of the theories and principles of the alternative model.[4]

According to our analysis, research on the two ideal types of sexual-affective relationships (the traditional and the alternative models) could discover the characteristics associated with love. This research could also discover how we make decisions about attraction and/or choice, which people are more successful and why, what people like the most about these successful individuals, which values we share with our friends, who influences us the most, what role families play, our ideal love story, and how we experience real love stories. In addition, such research could explore the frequency and depth of our peer-group discussions; how much we search for passion and/or stability; the degree to which we value respect, sincerity and nonviolent relationships; the type of image that we project; and the actions we take to project a specific image. Furthermore, research could determine the degree to which we value being attractive, who makes the decisions in each relationship, how the media influence us, who we have had relationships with, and what attracted us in those people. Finally, such research could shed light on how often we choose through reasoning and how often we choose "spontaneously" and how we resolve problems in relationships as well as the level of responsibility that we demonstrate, the degree of autonomy we develop, and the level of initiative with which we act. All these questions will be discussed in the following chapter.

· 4 ·

THE VOICES OF ADOLESCENTS

This research was carried out in order to ascertain how adolescents find meaning in their actions, construct their social reality and desires, and interact in and communicate about sexual-affective relationships. This study has opened the door to the transformation of loving attraction, greater choice in loving relationships, and sexual-affective action guided by reflection and dialogue in search of a relationship that unites stability and passion at the same time and with the same person.

The new coeducational proposals seem to facilitate this pathway, although they have significant inadequacies. We still don't know whether adolescents choose to have relationships with people who have the values recommended by transformative educational proposals or those who have negative and exclusionary values. Do egalitarian relationships inspire passion in adolescents, or do they lead to friendship without passion? Can adolescents achieve a relationship that is full of both stability and passion with the same person? Do they believe that tastes and desires are unchangeable, or do they consider how to transform them?

The data here were collected from girls and boys in compulsory secondary education (12 to 16 years of age). First relationships hold great significance, as they can satisfy or destroy the most ambitious dreams. When two young people travel down the path of being in love, including all stages of devotion, affection, and passion (a path on which sincerity, equality, and emotions represent signs of identity), their lifestyle differs to a great degree from that of those who use, despise, deceive, and/or mistreat [others]. In other words, young people can learn how to avoid dissatisfaction instead of learning how to repair its damages. Therefore, I examined the type of people (according to their values) that young people choose when they establish relationships. However, as will be shown, the results of this study can be easily recognized in a sample of another age group.

The general objective of the research is to determine whether coeducational efforts, alternative educational practices, and the progress of feminism have ensured that girls and boys in compulsory secondary education feel attraction to and choose people who have transformative and progressive values based on the alternative model of sexual-affective relationships or whether they feel attracted to and choose those who have the values of the traditional model (womanizers, women who imitate the traditional model of masculinity, and stable passionless couples).[1]

My perspective is communicative, which coincides with the theoretical bases, methodological principles, and criteria that are considered valid by the international scientific community.[2] Scientific knowledge is produced through a type of intersubjectivity that understands social reality to be a construction. The significance of this construction is generated through interaction and mutual comprehension and based on critical reflection and self-reflection. We aim to not only describe, understand, and/or analyze the sexual-affective reality but also to contribute lines of action that will transform the different contexts or realities that we participate in in order to yield results with social utility.

I collected information using multiple techniques, including communicative focus groups, communicative life stories, and a literature review. I carried out the first two life stories and communicative groups to determine the actions, interpretations, meanings, dialogue, and debates carried out among the studied population. I studied *Ragazza*, a magazine for young girls with a wide readership, and contrasted it with a magazine for adult women, *Cosmopolitan*. I used content analysis to analyze the information. I classified as exclusionary all phenomena that led to the reproduction of the system and had negative repercussions on young people – "instinctive" love, a lack of respect, violence, selfishness, a lack of reflection, instrumental rationality, a lack of responsibility, etc. I classified as transformative all phenomena that worked to overcome those exclusionary elements – stable and passionate love, independence, affection, solidarity, respect, egalitarian dialogue, communicative rationality, responsibility, etc. A clear predominance of the exclusionary was considered to be due to the traditional model. In the transformative case, action was the result of progressive values as reflected by the alternative model.

Voices from magazines

The monthly magazine *Ragazza* has a target audience of adolescents between the ages of 12 and 18 and is typically read by young girls in compulsory secondary school. In this study, we primarily focused on the section titled "Unashamed," which was later retitled "Confidential." In 2003, "Hugo's Advice" was added to this section. We reviewed issues from 1998 to 2003 from various years and we monitored and classified the information. The information was divided into exclusionary and transformative data based on the positioning and attitudes of the people who wrote to the magazine as well as the position of the magazine itself.

In *Ragazza*, love was typically defined as a bolt of lightning or "chemistry" rather than the result of one's own decision or choice: "Love is like an arrow which goes in through your eyes and when it reaches the heart it explodes like fireworks" (June 2002: 12). In addition, there are lots of relationship quizzes that associate love with the magic that reaches you suddenly from Cupid's arrow (February 2002; June 2002; December 2002). The following statement of a young male actor from a famous Spanish television series is significant: "It is difficult for me to be faithful. I have no patience! (…) My brain is in total chaos" (August 98: 40).

It is also typical of the traditional model the way concepts in the magazine such as risk and passion and security and romanticism are paired: passion is associated with risk, and there is no suggestion that a relationship could be both secure and passionate or romantic and risky at the same time: "Laid-back, soft hearted, hard hearted… What are you like when you're in love? What makes you quiver: risks or safety, romanticism or passion? Discover it now" (February 2002: 87). Interest in a person is linked to obtaining that person through conquest. Once this goal is achieved, it seems logical for a lack of motivation to arise. Faced with this situation, the magazine provided advice such as "don't worry because it's normal," without suggesting any reason to change, simply "trust blindly" in the fact that the day will come when "finally" a boy or girl will become "desirable" (December 2000; June 2002). The magazine even promoted relationships and desires that were based on jealousy (March 2001).

Furthermore, on occasions when flings that could lead to disaster were sought (for example, [girls] wanted to date older boys who "ignored" them for two years), the magazine suggested both using another group of guys to determine whether the girls could achieve their objective or the girls taking the first step in addressing those boys without analyzing why the girls found them attractive:

…they only come over to us when they are drunk or they are bored.

Answer: Those guys see that you are so into them and they are so sure that you will chase after them (…) get together with another group of guys (…) if they want to get you, they have to put more effort in (July 2000: 91).

Transformative attitudes were displayed on only a few occasions (March 2001; February 2003; May 2003; July 2003). These attitudes involved undertaking a process of reflection when facing a betrayal and having a critical and self-critical attitude. However, the magazine has recently improved in regard to the expression of transformative attitudes:

They told me that my best friend is involved with my boyfriend, and I don't know what to do…

Answer: Before you act, the first thing you have to do is to make sure you are well-informed. Do you fully trust the person who said this to you? …The best thing is for you to talk to them…If this happens we recommend that you immediately swap your friend for someone else, and as far as he is concerned, someone who is capable of acting like that does not deserve to be with you! (February 2003: 81–82)

I can deduce that apart from the fact that the traditional model continues to prevail, sexism is deeply rooted. We continue to desire and choose the most attractive women and the men who have the most power. This long-standing and clear attitude resists change.

On many occasions, nonegalitarian relationships tend toward dependence:

I have been going out with a guy (…) he's broken up with me three times (…) In the end he left me for good and, on the school trip, he made out with a foreign girl in front of me (…) this made me decide to go out with another guy. The truth is that

I don't love my current boyfriend as much as I loved my "ex" (...) my ex boyfriend has recently been acting as if he wants us to get back together. (December 2000: 97)

The response from the magazine erroneously focused the problem on the current boyfriend rather than addressing the problem of attraction and choice: "...If this is happening to you, perhaps it is because your current boyfriend is not ideal, and maybe you need someone else" (December 2000: 97).

Examples that referenced kisses were quite frequent. The magazine argued that a specific person "is a better kisser," connecting a desire to date a person with good kissing techniques:

Three weeks ago I met Rafa and started to date him. However, after two weeks he broke up with me. I wasn't really that bothered to be honest. Yesterday I made out with David and, when he kissed me, I thought about Rafa, and about how good he was at kissing me. What can I do? I don't want David to suffer because of me. (January 2001: 90)

As demonstrated in the magazine, a lack of solidarity in loving relationships is not surprising. Betrayal and a lack of consideration for the other person are common situations in sexual-affective relationships: "My ex-boyfriend made out with my sister right in front of my nose when we were dating. I still like him (...) but (...) If he wants anything he'll have to work for it" (December 2000: 97).

Disrespect in a relationship leads to the inability to talk about love or affection, as it indicates selfishness and a lack of interest in other people's feelings. One of the most common situations reported in *Ragazza* is when a boy aims to take advantage of a girl, does so, and then puts her down:

He asked me if I was a virgin, I said I was, and he replied that it was about time that I lost my virginity (...) He wanted to take my shirt off and I said no (...) in the end I found myself with my bra undone while he continued to touch and kiss me. I felt like making love with him, but I don't know, something held me back (...) When we went back to the group, he acted as if nothing had happened between us (...) apparently, the day after the absolute bastard told all of the guys in the group what he had done with me, down to the last detail. It has been very difficult for me to get rid of that reputation (...). (September 2000: 108)

Many quotes in the magazine demonstrated the desire to make out with people who transmitted an image of being hot, a flirt, etc. at first meeting. Girls did not question these people's values. Rather, they asked how to hit on these desired individuals, thus hurtling toward betrayal and pain: "I like this guy

(…) he is really cute and a bit bigheaded. The other day, one of my guy friends told me that the guy wants to make out with me (…) What do you think I need to do to make out with him?" (August 1998: 84). This situation seems easy to identify and simple to avoid; however, when we actually face it, it puts us in a quandary.

Another common problem is the lack of respect that occurs when people in a relationship are playing a double game. A teenager had a girlfriend but decided to conquer a friend of his girlfriend. Rather than rejecting him and exposing the boy's double game, the friend focused her efforts on trying to date the boy:

> In my gang there's this guy who's really cute, and he's dating this girl. I really like him and I think he likes me too. When he's with his girlfriend he ignores me, but when she goes home he is very affectionate to me. How can I make him mine? (December 2002: 88)

One figure that frequently appeared was the "understanding" partner who was forgiving when his/her boyfriend or girlfriend left them for a more attractive individual. But when those who have strayed realize that the new relationship is a "farce" and want to get back with their original partners, the latter forgive the unfaithful ones and welcome them back with open arms:

> I left Juan too, a really nice guy and a really good person (…) to go back to an ex who had been unfaithful to me several times. What was the result? Well, we lasted for one weekend. Luckily Juan is very understanding and he believed me when I said that I had realized the kind of bastard that my ex is. (December 2000: 97)

These situations involve repeated betrayals; therefore, the magazine should emphasize not only the regret and understanding but also clear communication so that the "understanding" partner (who knows that they may not arouse passion but that the "bastard" does) can change his/her attitude if he or she does not want this situation to repeat itself.

The desire for people to like us, especially those who we like, is fundamental. However, it would be counterproductive and disturbing if those who wished to be liked accepted the magazine's suggestion: "You say 'Do you want to make out with me' Yes…You put them on cloud nine if…Tell me how good a dancer they are and I'll tell you how good they are in bed…" (January 2002: 78). In addition, the magazine provided abundant recommendations for how to be successful as the hottest girl of the night or the party, thus promoting competitiveness (August 2002; December 2002).

The magazine's advice columns placed a greater value on strategies than dialogue. In the case of betrayal, although they did provide some useful advice, in general, the advisors leaned toward tactics such as "making them beg you" before discussing dialogue and communication. Such advice might impede people from in-depth discussions about such problems:

> My boyfriend confessed to me that during the holidays he made out with a girl, but that he wants to continue dating me. I know that he has been truthful, but I am in a mess. What should I do?

> Answer: …anyone can make a mistake (…) It wouldn't be a bad idea to make him beg you a bit…Then, you'll realize how in love with you he is. (October 2002: 100)

Imposition and lies (September 2000; December 2000; February 2001) do not help to build relationships based on respect and trust. Rather, they generate tension and deny people the opportunity to discuss the situation so they can understand it: "…a friend of mine said to me that he's messing with all the girls, and, on top of that, I have caught him out in a couple of lies. Can I trust him? Should I meet up with him again if he calls me?" The magazine's response was strange: "…tell him what [kind of relationship] you would like to have with him (…) Make it very clear to him that he does not have to decide at that moment, but he also needs to know that you will not be waiting around eternally for him to make his mind up…" (August 1998: 84–85).

Based on the magazine's content, consideration for the other person is not one of the editorial strong points, at least in sexual-affective relationships. The writers did not demonstrate a desire to consider how to solve the problems, improve relationships, or change the motivation. Faced with these situations in relationships, the magazine's responses did not promote the need to respect the feelings of the other person involved. Rather, the magazine stated that the problem was a bad patch, habit, or routine:

> …Think about the fact that you have been together for a long time, and that, perhaps you are going through a bad patch (…) However, be careful, it may also be that, since you have been with him for so long, you are continuing the relationship out of habit and through a fear of being alone. (January 2001: 90)

On other occasions, the magazine's explanations involved "chemistry" or magic: "(Love) spells are always efficient as long as they have the intention of doing good" (February 2002: 79).

On the other hand, in reference to homosexuality and heterosexuality, the magazine's editorial position was that people are continuously changing, modifying their preferences, and reflecting and reacting according to external influences. In other words, it presented a transformative argument that involved criticism of the exclusion or marginalization of those who are different and defended people's sexual freedom: "As individuals we construct our sexual orientation from the moment we are born, to the moment we die. There are people who (...) change their preferences at a certain point in their life (...) don't worry, you will find out in time" (December 2000: 96). Situations of potential homosexuality in which a lack of thoughtfulness and dialogue placed a friendship in jeopardy were criticized:

> My friend Lorena and I (...) were inseparable. She used to spend the day telling me how pretty I am, and she would grab me by the hand or by the waist. I didn't pay any attention, because she was my best friend. The bad thing is that she started to do it (...) at school (...) she said that she wanted to make out with me, just to try it out! (...) She said that it was a joke (...) I started to avoid meeting up with her... (November 2000: 87)

With regard to rationality, the magazine typically promoted the exclusionary dimension, as it recommended acting on intuition, destiny, and hunches rather than reason: "...you should forget about prejudices and allow yourself to be led by your intuition and be, perhaps a bit less rational (...) If you allow yourself to be led by your hunches, then love will be your lottery [win]" (December 2000: 98). This perspective associates passion, dreams, and magic with the unknown, letting oneself go, and destiny: "What I want is a normal girl, passionate...You know? I believe in destiny and, when she appears, I will know it is her" (November 2002: 46). Thus, careful reflection on one's behavior and the imperative of rationality in love and feelings were not promoted. There were many examples of the typical conception of sexual relationships, not in terms of feelings but in terms of something physical (January 2001; January 2002; March 2002), such as the way in which the person moved, danced, etc. "I am so crazy about her. At first I wasn't sure at all, but as soon as she kissed me...She drove me crazy!" (September 1998: 38).

One case involved a relationship between a Roma boy and a non-Roma girl that ended despite their wish to continue the relationship. Clear indications of racism among the girl's peer group, in her family, and in the school environment in general led to a lack of dialogue and a subsequent break-up.

The decisions were one-sided, instrumental, impulsive. The lack of communication and conflicting power claims ended the relationship:

> I met a really nice new guy at school (...) I felt great when I was with him. However, my friends didn't like him one little bit, because he is Roma (...) money disappeared from a school bag (...) Juan started to have a really bad reputation and so did I (...) My parents took it really badly and wanted to force me to leave him (...) I decided to run away from home and escape with my boyfriend (...) they caught us and took us back to Madrid (...) my father was much stronger than I was, and he managed to destroy my relationship. He moved me to a different school (...) the bad atmosphere with my parents defeated my love for Juan. I know that I'll never forgive them. (October 2002: 102)

This is one of the few examples that were linked to ethnic origin, but it demonstrates how racism negatively influences sexual-affective relationships.

We also analyzed specific passages from *Cosmopolitan* for young adults. Superficial relationships were abundantly presented in this magazine:

> On one occasion, I was in a bar with a friend, Inma, and I said something that was not very original: "Let's go out on the make! (...) look into their eyes in a flirtatious way, don't talk about anything important, they don't look like they'd put up with it." (July 2000: 16)

At times, such passages revealed habitual behavior patterns: "I am not able to describe my nights out on the make, because, to be honest I can't keep count of them (...) I like to go out, to flirt and to make out with the guys I like" (July 2000: 19).

Attractive men were sought to make out with:

> I chose a really cute one who was in a group of guys and we were both looking at each other (...) I would say that I got the hot one because I kissed him without hesitation by making this ingenious statement: "I bet my friend that I would dare to kiss you. Will you let me win?" So he let me. (July 2000: 16)

This quote illustrates a typical encounter: "I met Ricardo one night, when I was out having a drink. There was a real spark between us. The night ended as one would expect: drinks, talking and [him] asking for my number" (July 2001: 16).

It was also common to make out with friends' boyfriends or husbands, thus betraying friends: "I went with my best friend's boyfriend. It only happened once and the truth is that we were both quite drunk. Should I tell my friend?"

(May 2003: 40). "I have a group of female friends and recently I found out that one of them is sleeping with the husband of one of the other girls. I haven't told the wife, but the situation is becoming very annoying. Should I tell the person involved or stay quiet?" (September 2002: 40). It was also common to have sex with husbands who constantly deceived their wives: "When he confessed to me that he was married, I had already been sucked into the situation. I have never thought that he might leave his wife and I don't even want him to" (July 2001: 16). These situations confirm an alarming lack of solidarity among women.

Meaningless one-night stands were considered natural: "I enjoy one-night stands at the time without questioning myself, nor do I ask whether we'll call each other the next day nor about what the guy thinks of me (…) one-night stands are simply fun (…) because I know it's only sex" (July 2000: 19).

It also appeared that questions of sex and love were not based on reason and choice but were just accepted as they arose: "In bars, at certain times of the night, for unexplained reasons, it seems that only short-term relationships occur, for one night or even two, with any luck" (July 2000: 16). "For months, every time I meet up with him, I think that this will be our last date, but when his number appears on my cell phone again, my heart flips and I end up putting off my plans to break up [with him]" (July 2001: 16). "I have thought about it a lot, and have come to the conclusion that it must be something hormonal. Maybe I have too many male hormones, just like men (…) the way I set things up for myself, there is not enough time for them to get to know me at all. That is, if a one night thing is all it is, then let it stay that way" (July 2000: 19).

In short, sex without feelings and deceit were advocated, justifying a lack of respect, a lack of solidarity, and an instrumental use of rationality. This trajectory has been demonstrated in the research over a period of years. Thus, the current discussion does not refer to coincidence. Rather, it reflects what occurs on a daily basis in the lives of many men and women.

We also examined the magazine's editorial comments (as is also true in the case of *Ragazza*). As observed below, although the writing in *Ragazza* was mainly categorized as the exclusionary dimension (although elements of the transformative dimension were found), *Cosmopolitan*'s exclusionary content greatly surpassed that of the adolescent magazine. For example, in answering a question from a woman who knew that her friend was sleeping with a friend's husband, the advice given by *Cosmopolitan* was:

Supposing you are absolutely sure and you feel morally obligated to do something about it, talk to the lover, not to the wife (…) possibly, her fear at knowing that the relationship is in the public domain will encourage them to put an end to it. If that's the case, forget about it, don't ever say a word about it to anyone or pay any attention to gossip or comments. However, if (…) your friend comes to you in search of consolation, don't increase her distress by telling her that you and other people were in the picture about what was going on. (September 2002: 40)

In addition, in reply to a woman who deceived her best friend, *Cosmopolitan* responded as follows:

There are some people who think that sincerity is the greatest virtue. I do not agree (…) your friend's boyfriend and you did something stupid, thoughtless and reprehensible. What will you gain by telling her about what happened? (…) you would hurt her a great deal and you would possibly destroy her relationship with her boyfriend and, of course, the friendship that you currently share (…) if she finds out what went on, she might become infuriated with her boyfriend and make a scene. However, in the end, even if the relationship is damaged, she will definitely forgive him. The person she will have no mercy on is you. Therefore, stay quiet and pray that he also does so. (May 2003: 40)

It is astonishing that the magazine promoted attitudes such as "forget about it"; "there are some people who think that sincerity is the greatest virtue. I do not agree"; and "stay quiet and pray that he also does so." In other words, a healthy relationship based on sincerity, equality, and feeling seemed to be inappropriate. The acceptance and concealment of lies, inequality, and a lack of solidarity and respect were promoted. This is an excellent reflection of the traditional model of sexual-affective relationships and double standards. In this aspect, as mentioned above, this magazine was inferior to *Ragazza*, in which alternative and/or critical approaches were more frequently found.

However, our analysis of *Ragazza* (as compared to *Cosmopolitan*) demonstrated that young people connect attraction to what is difficult to get and which they find impossible to analyze or understand. The magazine referred to spells, rituals, magic, and supernatural powers, linking love with magic (in a large number of reader quizzes) and stating that it is beyond our decision-making powers. Love was associated with a bolt of lightning or "chemistry" rather than a decision or choice. Furthermore, risk was linked to passion, romanticism to security, and motivation was only relevant to the conquest. The magazine more often than not advised people to act based on intuition, destiny, hunches, "letting oneself go," and "chemistry" than on reason. Therefore, it avoided not only reflection but also rational choice by only focusing on physical appeal, technique-related and superficial issues. The editorial advice promoted relationships based on jealousy and the use of peer groups of girls and boys to achieve the objective of hitting on [and then discarding] a desired person. At the same time, the magazine promoted the idea of taking the first step without an in-depth analysis of the reasons why the chosen person was desired. Individualistic and deceptive thoughts and behavior were viewed as normal. The lack of solidarity among girls was especially significant, as girls dated their friend's or even their sister's boyfriend or husband.

The magazine contained many passages in which flirtations with "hot" boys and girls were sought, without any questions about these individuals' values. The magazine even highlighted the "understanding" partner, whose partner had left them for a more "attractive person, came back, and was welcomed with open arms." Likewise, the magazine presented a common situation – faced with certain unwanted proposals that were accompanied by strong pressure, it may be highly difficult to object to them. These cases were highlighted through prolonged discussions and comments such as "when a girl says no, she really means yes" that permitted the boy to force the girl, who first objected but later submitted.

Few transformative attitudes that involved a process of reflection and a critical and self-critical attitude were found in *Ragazza*. Basically, the most positive aspect that the magazine provided good advice about the need for sincerity and communication, about loving oneself and knowing that, because a couple's experience involves two people, couples must agree in decisions. However, such advice was not usually provided, as exemplified by the discussion of kissing. The basic point was that knowing how to kiss is important, making it logical to suggest that one should date "good kissers." Neither teenagers who wrote to the magazine nor the writers for the magazine clarified that kisses, caresses, and other demonstrations of affection and passion find their meaning in the feelings in a relationship. They did not discuss an emphasis on talking and feeling rather than the use of unusual techniques. They also did not mention that "being a good kisser" tends to correspond to a certain attitude that involves confidence and control and perhaps leads to subsequent deceit and indifference, violence, etc.

The magazines analyzed clearly demonstrated not only that attraction and choice lead to the exclusionary values of the traditional model but also that the magazines (by expressing the traditional attitudes of the media) reflect the general preference for the values related to that model. Thus, simulated love, deceit, a lack of respect, instrumental rationality, and a great lack of solidarity became the common denominators.

Voices from communicative life stories

In all of the life stories, the attraction model was clearly defined, and the differences between the genders were confirmed. Some of these definitions of attraction were (for example, and only in the case of boys) those who were *show offs* and *arrogant*, those who emanated *strength*, and those who were *bad* to girls.

> *R3:* However, the physical thing, what does that mean? (…)
> *P3:* Strength really, and showing off (…), yes, arrogance.
> *P16:* [who is] the boy who is the most successful? (…) Well in my group, it's clearly Miquel. Really because of his personality. Because he's a guy who's really open, very outgoing (…) he gets very close to them [girls], and he gets their number.

Girls were basically attracted to physical characteristics. Statements such as those who "are hot, those who have the best bodies, the cute ones," and so on were made. Other aspects of the person, such as *friendliness* or being bright or *snobs*, were also added: P2: "The hottest ones, no? The ones who have the best bodies (…) who are cute (…), I don't know…whatever people usually say."

Friends were generally the nice guys who treated the girls properly and who, according to the traditional model of attraction, were not desired. Meanwhile, the boy who was a *show-off or arrogant* and/or treated girls badly created excitement and was considered more attractive:

> *P11:* A friend does not attract you like…because it's a friend, you know? He's your friend, not your boyfriend, it's different, to be honest (…) you never have that intention because you don't go around with the sneaky idea that he likes you.
> *R:* So, why do we choose those who may lie to us and treat us badly?
> *P15:* Well…it's that thing inside, it's love at first sight and all of that. What we [girls] like is love at first sight, the show-offs, the hot ones and that's it (…) on the other hand, a good guy doesn't hit you like a lightning bolt and all that stuff.

Jealousy was often understood as a demonstration of love for another person. This type of relationship faithfully corresponds to the traditional model of attraction, which promotes competitiveness and inequality within the partnership:

> R: So, in the beginning, did you like the jealousy?
> P11: When I was engaged, I did like it because it was like nice jealousy. (…) Well [then the male partner made the following type of statements]: "I don't like you to dress like that" or something like that, you know? Well, you like it (…) Because you think: "See, he's looking at me…" you know? He doesn't like me to be looked at
> R: As if you were his girl…
> P11: exactly! …and you like it.

Novelty and variety were valued because they generated motivation. If these concepts are the fundamental bases of attraction, then once they disappear, indifference, routine, or boredom arises, eliminating all vestiges of passion. The following is another clear example of the strength of the traditional model:

> R: However, this can happen, no, that both people start out really enthusiastically…
> P10: Of course and then it goes (…) Like some of them say…they get tired of her, they say: "oh, I'm tired of her now.'"
> P12: I know people who have broken up but not because it was awful, but because it was over and they were getting bored, [well] they didn't know what to do anymore (…) Because it was all just routine and in the end, they were tired of it.

Some of the life stories brought up the risk of falling in love at first sight without any reflection. This type of choice is highly likely to be linked to the traditional model: P16: "I would say that there are different types of love (…) There is love at first sight, when you look at someone and you see that…you know? That there is a connection."

However, in the same individuals, we could find alternative positions that were transformative. These positions included the view that love must maintain passion and desire and that the passage of time does not imply the end of a relationship:

> P16: There can be passion but you can also feel very good with her because security is, I'm not quite sure how to say this…feeling good, no? To be in a situation where you feel fucking amazing you know? Being sure about what you're doing and knowing that the other person feels good with you. I think that is the ideal

situation, to be sure of yourself, of what you are doing, and of what she is doing. Feeling passion, and that is what you look for, no?

However, not only was it difficult to find quotes like these, but also the transformative statements that we found corresponded to situations that were not real but only desires. That is, the adolescents were not discussing their experiences but what they would like to experience: P12: "I don't know, maybe the fact that people have been together for a while and it is [still] like the beginning, for example. That it hasn't changed in time. "

The boy who was the most sought after and the girl who was the most popular played an important role. The people who surround the adolescents influenced each other by marking the attraction that the adolescents felt towards a specific person, thus losing their independence: P1: "If one girl likes him…well then, all of them like him, and if no girls like him, then none of them like him (…) because if one of them thinks he's hot, then the others think he's hot. And, if one girl thinks he's ugly, the others will think he's ugly too."

It was considered normal for people who were treated well and showered with attention to say that they were being *smothered*. In the life stories, affection was never associated with attraction, desire, or passion. Rather, the opposite was true, highlighting the difference between people's perceptions of their ideal relationship and their actual actions and feeling. Most adolescents expressed a desire for a relationship in which affection and respect were predominant. However, they felt attracted to people who could not fulfill this desire:

R: How would you like a guy to treat you? (…)
P1: Nicely but without suffocating me (…) being there for me but without being too much (…) I like people to chase after me, but I also like to chase after them.

The adolescents typically considered conflict in couples to be within the exclusive confines of their relationship. Thus, when faced with problematic situations, even gender violence, it was difficult for friends to intervene. The lack of solidarity in these cases was viewed as consideration for the partner, as not "interfering."

R: And if the couple has a problem, do you all try to help them or do you think that it's between the two of them?
P3: It's between them.

The feeling of fun, excitement, and adventure was lost when the couple finally became *serious*. The most concerning issue is that the adolescents did not tend to actually experience these relationships, but they wished to experience them:

> P2:   I don't know, for a while, no? I think that, I don't know, when you're fifteen (…) it depends, if it's to get married and everything, well, you pay more attention, no? To the way they are and to everything.
>
> R: And if not?
>
> P2:   If it's just for a while then…just the fact that she's hot is enough.

Numerous examples illustrated that many girls endured boyfriends who did not respect them, were unfaithful, and did not make them feel valued. However, the girls continued to date these boys and to feel a strong attraction to them, which even "impeded" them from respecting themselves and influenced them to accept gender violence, deceit, and eventual rejection:

> P5:   When you're fourteen you meet a guy (…) you like him, but then you start to get to know him and it turns out that he is a bit of a bad-ass, so to speak. Even though he's a bad person, I don't know, you still like him, but in another way.
>
> R: Have you ever come across a situation in which one of your female friends was with a guy who treated her badly, or…?
>
> P9:   Yes, when they only paid attention to looks and nothing else, they use them (…) there is one who's going out with an older guy, he's twenty, and he's embarrassed to be going out with her, when he's with his friends, it's as if she doesn't exist (…) when they are alone, they're fine, but it embarrasses him when he's with his friends. She wouldn't like to admit that this is the case…

Image was strongly linked to models of attraction and choice. To be "successful" and liked, people carefully created an image, and [this image] differed for boys and girls. In this sense, although boys and girls carried out the same actions, their images largely differed. Girls who made out with a number of guys had a bad reputation, whereas boys that had a "long list of conquests" were considered successful. People liked and were attracted to these boys. Therefore, these boys were viewed as successful and fortunate. This was demonstrated by the pride obvious in some of the quotations:

> P12: If a girl makes out with lots of guys, then she's a whore…. On the other hand, a guy isn't, he's a winner.
>
> R: For example, the guy in your group of friends who makes out with loads of girls…what do you think of him?

P3:   Well, that he's a bastard and that he's very lucky. I have only messed around
        with approximately 30 of them, and the zero is not there for decoration
        (laughter) (…) I'm the one who gets more girls than anyone else.

P16:   When you've messed around with a girl and you talk about it with your friends,
        I don't know, it's as if they support you, and they say to you, "Fuck, man, what
        a stud" or things like that.

Girls who dated many guys and obtained a "bad reputation" were chosen
only for superficial, rash, sporadic or nonserious relationships. The same out-
come was evident for boys who had a certain arrogant attitude or *showed off*.
However, when looking for a relationship and reflecting on their future, some
girls chose boys who treat them well although they believed that they were
sacrificing the passion that they felt for the *show offs*, thus reinforcing the
traditional model: P15: "I like those type of guys, tough guys, show-offs, the
ones who have a good car, who look at you…But, later on, to be honest, really
everyone, when it's a guy to marry, well [you want] him to be a good guy, a
serious guy."

Some cases reflected the disappointment caused by relationships in which
the traditional model had left its mark, ensuring that all exclusionary situations were experienced as normal. Pessimism was expressed when the adolescents faced the difficulty of changing: P5: "Now, at sixteen, you see these
things differently, but at that time, well, I don't know, it gets to you too much
and it makes you feel really bad, you see everything as if…it's normal that
they might do something shitty to you, let's just say that it's not out of the
ordinary."

We observed quite a few examples of the strategies that the womanizers
used to obtain a girl. Often the peer group came into play. The womanizer
makes the girl feel that she is "the chosen one."

P10:   That's why I say it's bad to fall in love early, because if you fall in love too
        early, well then you can't (…) Well, depending on the girl, also. If the girl is,
        in my own words, an octopus girl (…).

R: What do you mean by an octopus girl?

P10:   That she will always be with one guy one day and another guy the next. But,
        oftentimes, an octopus woman is good. The strategy facilitates what you can
        do at any given time and who to achieve it with.

P5:   On the fifth day, let's say, at night, we started to play around a bit more and
        watched the sunrise. On the second last day, our classmates started to do the
        typical kidding around (…) so, in the afternoon, she said sorry for all of the
        things her classmates had said about her and then at night, well, after the
        party, at bedtime, we made out with each other.

The adolescents often decided to continue being with a person even though they realized that the person had negative values. According to the life stories, friends did not position themselves strongly against relationships that were traditional and negative: R: "Should they break off the relationship, especially the person being mistreated?" P3: "I would say so, but she says that she loves him too much to leave him."

In short, the life stories included content that was similar to that found in *Ragazza*. The attractive boys were *show offs, arrogant, strong,* and *bad* to girls (the friend is concerned, good, but not desired), while the attractive girls were *the hot ones, those who had the best bodies, and the cute ones, as well as those who were nice, smart and stylish.* The adolescents identified love with a lightning bolt and viewed jealousy as a demonstration of love, thus promoting competitiveness and inequality. *Ragazza* underlined the fact that desire came to an end once the conquest was complete. In the life stories, we saw that novelty and variety generated motivation. If these disappeared, the result was indifference, routine, and boredom, thus eliminating passion. Security was linked to a loss of fun and adventure, implying that one wants to have fun in the midst of insecurity at a certain age, and older people may decide to settle for a boring future.

These life stories clearly reflected that many girls endured mistreatment, rejection, and/or deceit because they could not say no to an "irrational" attraction. These girls endured infidelity and violence and were willing to endure any mistreatment to continue the relationship. On the other hand, and no less significantly, these girls did not pay attention to, much less fall in love with, those who treated them well.

Some alternative transformative positions were also found. These positions involved the understanding that love requires passion, desire, and affection over time and that these are the ingredients of loving relationships. Nevertheless, these positions were related to situations that did not yet exist, but they were desired. This is reflected by the fact that people claimed to feel *smothered* when others showed them care and attention.

Voices from communicative focus groups

In general, the focus groups reported various elements that we observed in both the communicative daily life stories and in *Ragazza*, although the magazine results were more troubling. The dialogue in the peer group ensured that each question debated in the focus groups was thoroughly addressed. Once the adolescents' experiences were reported, each subject was addressed in a more reflexive manner. This allowed for the discussion of facts (rather than what people would like to do), something less specific than the communicative daily life stories.

There is little to say about the numerous definitions of love and attraction that were recorded in the four communicative focus groups. The adolescents debated the characteristics of boys who were attractive (or not attractive) while taking it for granted that girls are considered attractive if they are beautiful. The *bad* boys drew attraction because they *turn you on, like a good time*, and *ignore girls*. In other words, those with the least respect [for girls] were viewed as attractive. Furthermore, boys were aware that they had to act in this specific manner to be successful:

R: Do you think that there are bad guys who people are attracted to, or even very attracted to?

G[4]2.3: Yes.

G2.2:   Yes. (…)

G2.1:   All of the girls I have spoken to [have said] the more of a bad boy he is…

G2.4:   The more they like him

G2.1:   The more they love him. (…) Because he turns them…he turns them on you know? (laughter)

G2.4:   Because they like a good time, it's true!

G2.3:   If they think that you're too much of a goody-goody, they say: "Ah I got that guy, I started to like him, and now I can do whatever I like with him"; but if they think you're a tough guy, if they think you're a bad boy, then they say "whoa."'

G2.2:   The more of a bad guy they are, the more we [girls] like them.

G2.1:   If he's all over you…(…)

G2.2:   That's it, the more of a bad boy they are, the more we like them because, if they boss us around or ignore us, then we like them more.

G.2.1: If at first sight, you see a shy guy you say: "oh what a jerk," but if you see that he's a show-off, you say: "oh, look at that one!" no matter how ugly he is.

G2.3:   I'm taking notes.

This concept has become so widespread that *mysterious, different* guys are sought because they represent irresistible attraction:

GI.3:   Well, the fact that they're mysterious.

G1.1:   Because the majority of the ones who ignore us are mysterious, and you want to find out about the mystery. You are intrigued, you know?

Being "the chosen one" is an important element of attraction in the traditional model. The strategic male flirt knows that this tactic generally attracts girls; therefore, he acts to reinforce this idea. The communicative focus groups confirmed that this is the case: G3.3: "We like to see that he chooses us out of everyone."

In addition, the girls' objective was to change the strategic male and his values. They wanted him to become another person and to stop acting in his typical manner. The girls wanted to change the very characteristics that attracted them:

G3.2: Maybe they can change, if they love you, they can change

R: Do you think the show-offs can change? (…)

G3.1: Yes, yes, if you want them to…its difficult, no? However, if…you work hard on it.

G3.2: If you work hard…(…)

G3.3: Yes, yes if you get him to fall in love with you…he changes.

G3.1: You have to be very serious about it…and work hard. I think that you can change him.

G3.2: (…) That is, try to, try to by every means possible.

Despite the fights and lack of respect, some people were unable to end a relationship based on "irrational" attraction:

G4.2: Yes, they get annoyed with each other, they break up, but then they get back together again, and it's like that all the time.

G4.1: I don't know, I think that they're hooked on each other by now, I don't know. I think that it's attraction, that as soon as you see him… I don't know.

The opposite was true in the case of the boy who people did not like and were not attracted to. As was mentioned at various times throughout the focus groups, the male friend was neither attractive nor liked. He was viewed as the type of person who loves you and treats you well and who you turn to when you need advice, help, or a shoulder to cry on. In fact, being good and devoted was identified with being weak, boring, and having no "charm;" in short, his virtuous characteristics were not attractive:

G4.3: Well, I always say something to her, or her, or to Celia or Sergio, for instance, and I say: "Look at what's happened to me again."

R: Who's Sergio?

G4.1: Sergio…

R: Whoa, that one's famous, eh?

G4.2: Very famous
G4.1: That's what we were saying to you, that he's a really good guy, he's really nice but his looks…

Although the relationships were not long term, people became excessively attached to their partner. This dependence, which made it difficult to leave the relationship and fed the terror of being alone, was derived from this "irrational" attraction toward a certain type of individual:

G4.3: If I could choose…well [someone who] would care about me.
R: And why do you think that you cannot choose?
G4.3: Well, it's because I am already quite attached to a guy already.
R: You are pretty hooked on him?
G4.3: Damn!

The problem of falling in love with a person who was at first perceived as a certain type but was later found to not be that type also arose. Interestingly, regardless of whether the adolescents were deceived or not, they were trapped and dependent:

R: How would the love be, then?
G4.1: Little by little, just little by little, you, I don't know, you fall in love with that person, and in the end, you realize that it is not what you thought it would be but…it gotcha!

The advice and viewpoints of the people who interacted with the adolescents didn't seem to aid them in forming opinions, shaping independence, or making the right decisions:

G4.1: I think that we always ask them for advice but we never pay attention to them. Whether it's your friend, your sister, or your mother. You always talk to them, but then you do whatever you want to do. I think that it's useful to unburden yourself, but it doesn't make you do anything about it. Well, maybe it helps.

The difficulty of dating a person who typically plays the role of the "tough guy" tends to increase one's desire for him and to move away from affection. This exclusionary concept of love that avoids affection was repeated throughout the focus groups:

R: And would it not be easier to go out with someone who is not like that?
G3.1: Someone passive?

> G3.3:   You always like tough guys. It is the difficulty of it that we like (…). The more
> difficulty it is, the more we like them.
> G3.1:   The less attention they pay to you, the more…
> G3.3:   The more [of a] bastard they are to us, the more we like them.
> G3.1:   Later on, the nicest thing is when they pay attention to you.

Fights were viewed as a normal aspect of a relationship and even as ways to inject excitement into a relationship. The lack of fights indicated a lack of *joy* and that the couple was becoming bored and had entered into a routine. This concept marked the great separation between passion and affection in such a way that reconciliatory sex following a fight was popular, motivated people, and was even sought after:

> R: And why do couples fight so much?
> G4.1:   I think that they have no reasons, people just seek them in everything. At
> least, I do.
> R: It seems like we say to ourselves: 'it's been awhile since we fought, and it
> seems like it's time now'.
> G4.1:   (laughter) It does happen sometimes, yes. In my opinion, if it doesn't, then
> something is missing (…)
> R: And then, the reconciliation, is that good?
> G4.1:   Yes.
> R: That kiss is like, more,…?
> G4.1:   Yes.
> R: And it happens when we've had a period which is very calm and it seems like
> something is missing…
> G4.1:   Joy (laughter).

The traditional model of attraction and choice incorporates a series of negative dynamics and concepts. One of these concepts, a lack of solidarity among women, is common. This is only to be expected because the prize they are competing for is the feeling of being "the chosen one." This only occurs when the boy states that out of all [of the girls], he is choosing one. This process generates competitive dynamics and increases the lack of solidarity:

> G3.3:   However, we are always attracted by something that we see and later we say,
> "Well, look, I have achieved this because I did something, because I earned
> it" (…)
> G3.1:   We like all those guys who have a lot of girlfriends.
> G3.3:   Then, I got him.
> G3.1:   And then you can say, "I got him because I'm better than all the rest of you"
> (…) And we like them to pay attention to one of us because, because we want

to demonstrate that we're worth something. Even if you don't marry him later, no? However, just because, 'You got him'."

A lack of respect – both on the part of the boys who act indifferently and may deceive or mistreat girls and the girls who lose their interest in and/or do not value the people who treat them well and care about them – was consistently demonstrated throughout the discussions. The following statement is one of the most transcendental aspects of the traditional model:

G4.1: When he feels like it, he keeps her for himself, when he feels like it. Yes, he ignores her completely, that is, he treats her like shit. But, she... (...). When it's in his interest, well, he fools around with her and she, well... [thinks it is] good. He makes out with whoever he wants, then he tells her, [but] she just ignores it. ...

Although the girls were aware that they were deceived and not highly respected, they did not change the balance of the relationships. Rather, they accepted these conditions and considered them to be an intrinsic part of relationships:

G4.1: (Laughter) Tell me about it. I don't know what I'll do. It's what I was saying before, that I don't know if the same thing was happening to me that was happening to her. When someone throws shit at me, well, I'll go back to them again.

At times, the attraction was produced by indifference, explaining why those who were not respectful were attractive:

G3.1: R: What do you like about guys? That they're hot...and, you know, kind of, show-off.

G3.2: When you see that they're ignoring you, well, you like that about them. When they pay a lot of attention to you...we don't like that so much about them...

G1.1: When you're always hanging around with someone, well, they don't pay attention to you, but if you ignore them, they do...That's true, and, why is that?

As it happened with the life stories, in the communicative focus groups a specific way of acting was associated with a certain reputation:

G4.1: A reputation...I don't know, when you're going around in your own way, from here to there, what I mean is, with one guy, or another. However, then, you see girls who are maybe going around with one guy and then another guy behind his back, and then they turn around and go with another guy, and mess around with everyone (…)

G4.2:   Maybe sometimes they think: "She's a whore"…

According to each boy's or girl's reputation and the labels that were attached to them as a result of their having (or not having) a lot of relationships, different classifications were established which accommodate themselves to the unequal types of relationships desired, always with gender difference as the key issue:

G2.1:   If she's full of life, if the girl is lively, if she's had a lot of guys, if she's had a long history with guys.

G2.2:   If they've had a lot of boyfriends or not because if they've had a lot of boyfriends, they like them more. Of course, more for just passing the time with, and if they're good [girls], well…

G2.1:   If they're good [girls], well they wise up.

G2.2:   Nooo. If they're good [girls], they wait for them so they can get married.

G2.1:   Yes. Or, sometimes, they're good and the boys wise them up and then don't want them anymore. Even if they're good, if they [the boys] turn them bad, then they turn bad and then they don't want to marry them anymore.

G2.2:   Just for a while, then that's it.

Appearance was important for boys but secondary to other traits such as attitude. Therefore, although boys increasingly attend to their physical appearance, they are aware that attitude is more important. The boys who have not been with many girls are written off as silly and dull:

R: It is different with guys than it is with girls?

G2.2:   Yes. Girls hide it but then maybe, then, the guys say so. The more girlfriends guys have, the better, and for girls, the fewer they have, the better. (…)

R: However, if it's a guy who has never been with a girl…

G2.2:   They call him a fag (laughter), or an asshole, one or the other.

G2.3:   No, maybe not a fag …

G2.4:   They treat him like an idiot, that is, that…they can already see that they can dominate him in any way they want to.

G2.1:   Because we don't say it to their face, but among ourselves [the girls], we do say it…

In a relationship based on the traditional model, egalitarian dialogue does not make people attractive:

G3.3:   We like to be told what to do and that's it.

G3.1:   We [girls] always want equality, but what we really like is to be told what to do.

G3.2: Yes, yes …lots of equality, but it depends what for.

G3.2: Yes, yes.

G3.3: Yes, equality, equality and then we like the people who dominate us.

The image that the young people projected had a large impact on choice. Therefore, they thought about and tried to manage their image, not only to have the desired relationships but also to choose who to settle down with:

G3.1: For a short-term thing, you seek the hot ones, the show-offs.

G3.2: And to, to, well for a longer thing with them, you can look for something more serious, I think (…) [it is important] that he's not a good-for-nothing, that he doesn't go out too much, […] serious…

G3.3: Of course, boys do the same thing. Firstly, they go around like I'm saying with the rebellious girl, and when they want to get serious, they go around with the ones [girls] who are serious, with the serious ones… (…)

R: And why is it important to go with a responsible one afterwards, when you want to get serious?

G3.3: Because he cheats on you.

G3.2: He cheats on you and it's…really bad (laughter).

G3.1: He goes to nightclubs.

In short, the groups were largely in agreement with the magazines and the life stories, but they did not identify a single transformative passage. The adolescents demonstrated a desire for sporadic relationships (for one or two nights) that did not consider feelings and were far removed from engagement and obligations. They experienced, understood, and accepted a lack of respect ("the less attention they pay you, the more you like them"), as it was a constitutive part of the relationship, strongly underlining the role of "the chosen girl," something that male strategists knew very well (the dynamics of competitiveness that are generated to conquer the "most sought-after" person or to feel that you are the "chosen girl"). In addition, adolescents attempted to change the person or the values of the "flirt" without solving the question of if they change the attractive characteristics of the other without changing themselves, they will lose interest in that person. They emphasized that people who treated others badly were desirable and that relationships with these people were not easily ended if bad behavior was followed by multiple apologies. Managing to get a "tough guy" and then fighting with him were viewed as not only normal but also desirable and necessary to prevent routine and boredom. I have seen that the adolescents were unable to end a relationship based on "irrational" attraction and found goodness and devotion to be negative attributes.

By way of reflection: In practice, the traditional model rules

My three sources of information all demonstrated that love: (1) is the most-discussed value; (2) is experienced in the most exclusionary way; (3) has social roots; (4) demonstrates the existence of sexism in the area of attraction and choice, as those who attract are the "tough guys" and the "hot girls"; (5) is based on "irrationality," spells, rituals, magic, "chemistry," instinct, etc.; and (6) indicates that choice and attraction are not addressed and/or debated in depth.

With regard to independence, the following traits were common: (1) relationships lean toward dependency because they are not egalitarian; (2) relationships based on lack of respect and humiliation create dependency; (3) relationships based on "irrationality" also create dependency; (4) the peer group can remove autonomy from the decisions of one group member; (5) independence is demanded in terms of the family, dialogue, and respect for people's own opinions; (6) the social role almost completely dominates, leaving little space for the role of the family and (7) it is easier for boys to act more independently than it is for girls.

Affection was observed in the magazine, life stories, and focus groups in the following ways: (1) the desire to get the "tough guy," the difficult one, leads to a relationship that lacks affection and has a tendency toward violence; (2) fights are viewed as normal, desirable, and necessary to break away from routine and boredom; (3) people are increasingly concerned with the physical or technical aspects of affection (how people kiss and the types of kisses and caresses) rather than feelings; (4) both girls and boys confuse the caresses of those who love them and treat them well with feelings of suffocation; and (5) affection and passion are not associated with the same person.

In relation to solidarity, the following points were observed: (1) there is a significant lack of solidarity in sexual-affective relationships; (2) the lack of solidarity among girls, especially when the most "sought-after" person or the feeling that one is "the chosen one" is at stake; (3) the only notable solidarity occurs within the peer group; and (4) both boys and girls confuse a lack of solidarity with simulated respect for the privacy of a couple that experiences conflict and/or gender violence.

The following results were found in relation to security or stability: (1) young people rarely discuss this value because they do not attach a great deal of significance to it; (2) many insecurities and fears that cannot be resolved based on sexual technique; (3) adolescents only associate security or stability with relationships that are "serious," and they view sporadic relationships as sources of enthusiasm, passion, and adventure; (4) adolescents link secure relationships with the arrival of obligations and a loss of fun and passion; and (5) adolescents can also view security as a sense of unconditional, permanent support and a value that provides balance.

With regards to respect, the following results were obtained: (1) as in the case of love, it is dangerous to allow one's emotions to be directed toward the wrong people; (2) there are many cases of boys who obtain girls and then humiliate and/or mistreat them; (3) the despised girls feel attracted to and become hooked on those who spurn them. According to the girls, this occurs "despite" insults and gender violence "because" the boys mistreat the girls and do not pay attention to them; (4) this situation is facilitated because people aim to flirt with those who attract them (encouraged by the media and the peer group); (5) girls not only face the abuse of those who treat them badly but also do not then become interested in those who treat them well; (6) the girl who "robs" a friend of her boyfriend is a common figure (this is linked to the lack of solidarity). Another often-encountered figure is the "understanding" partner who welcomes back the person who abandoned their relationship for a "mistaken" passionate relationship; (7) a dangerous lack of respect is experienced, understood, and accepted as part of the relationship; (8) however, respect should be present and relationships should be based on dialogue and consensus; and (9) the reaction of boys with progressive values to girls who treat these boys well and love them cannot be clarified here: Do these boys lose their interest and/or ignore these girls or become even more interested in them?

The following points concerning image were observed: (1) image is becoming more important every day; (2) concern about superficial image-related issues minimizes the significance of profound issues that involve feelings and values; (3) girls who date many boys have a bad reputation, whereas boys who date many girls have a good reputation; (4) girls aim to be attractive through beauty and boys through power; and (5) both boys and girls seek to promote their qualities in order to appear attractive.

With regard to communication, (1) there is a tendency to place a greater value on strategies than dialogue; (2) a relationship with egalitarian dialogue appears to be less attractive and motivating than a relationship in which one person (the male) is "in charge"; (3) in theory, adolescents believe that dialogue is the ideal mechanism to overcome conflict in a relationship; and

(4) a couple's conflicts are not typically resolved through dialogue, and the peer group and friends rarely intervene in a couple's fights.

The results concerning rationality were as follows: (1) rationality occupies a negative position, as there is either a lack of rationality in the relationship or only instrumental rationality is used; (2) adolescent relationships are guided by intuition, destiny, "chemistry," and instinct; (3) adolescent reasoning is instrumental. They use strategies to achieve the desired aim: when hitting on people, resolving conflict in a couple, influencing the peer group, talking to family, and so on; and (4) adolescents infrequently make decisions and behave based on communicative rationality.

With regard to making decisions, the following points were established: (1) decisions are made with the aim of obtaining the desired boy or girl at any cost, without concern for the means used or the type of relationship; (2) when strongly pressured, adolescents find it difficult to make their desired decision; (3) in making a decision about a new relationship, adolescents do not view past lifestyles and relationships as having a significant impact on them; and (4) if adolescents are "irrationally" attracted to a person who is jealous, aggressive, and violent, they will still continue the relationship.

The above conclusions summarized the experience of attraction and choice in accordance within the traditional model of relationships. In other areas, such as sexual freedom, clear progress has been made. However, in the area of attraction and choice, I have either not taken a step forward or have taken a step backward. This is evidenced by the statistics on gender violence as well as the resulting deaths and the fruitless search for relationships that are full of affection and passion. Where are the dreams and the enthusiasm? Although the panorama is clouded, we attempt to clarify it in the final chapter.

· 5 ·

CONCLUSIONS AND FUTURE PROSPECTS

Conclusions

First, we need to remind ourselves that the keys to addressing love in this new society are as follows:

1. *The radicalization of modernity.* Love no longer needs to be associated with instinct or anchored to the philosophy of consciousness. Rather, it incorporates intersubjectivity as a transformative element of the consequences of evolution and social change while seeming to be personal and private. The communicative force in current society guarantees that the traditional family institution cannot and allows us to move closer to the dream of loving passion.
2. *Social actors as protagonists.* We can now be the protagonists of our own lives through processes of individualization, overcoming the determinism of structuralism. We are faced with two fields of action, one communicatively structured and one formally organized. The structures of communication are now being liberated in families and educational settings, increasing opportunities for choice and freedom. The strength and normativity of the system are facts. However, the strength of our own protagonism is also a fact. We can rewrite our own destinies

through constant dialogue and communication in a quest for a loving relationship that includes both stability and passion.

3. *The role of dialogue and consensus.* What was previously done without negotiation must now be discussed and agreed upon. This discursive process establishes democracy in love that is not subject to government declarations, laws, debates, or voting in parliament but functions according to the lovers' desires and agreements. Although we observe and experience unequal positions of power in families, couples, and other relationships, dialogue is a better option than the traditional imposition of the will of the strongest. The new dynamic creates new spaces that entail communicative rationality so an argument has weight based on its validity rather than its author. Under these new conditions, loving passion between equals is possible. Otherwise, passion and love will remain separate, and rationality and emotion will be viewed as discordant.

4. *Re-enchantment in communication.* We no longer need to use language based on a specific aim. Rather, the aim can be established through dialogue, resulting in agreements and discussions based on equal conditions. When travelling along this path, our future will depend on whether we can correctly choose the person we fall in love with, whether we can ensure that gender equality does not lead to a lack of desire, and than we can find true liberation by redefining and reprogramming our tastes, preferences, attractions, and desires. In resolving such problems, love can gain a new meaning, causing us to become re-enchanted when we create a new life that corresponds to our current society. The relationship will exist while the feelings endure. For these feelings to endure, we must become elated through a new type of communication that unites love and passion as well as stability and "craziness."

For these keys to function correctly, they must be supported by theories and practices generated by a satisfactory process of attraction and choice. Although critical educational theories, proposals, materials, and exercises governed by values that differ from the traditional values exist, they do not provide an in-depth consideration of attraction and choice. Therefore, they are insufficient. In addition, agents of socialization (with the media at the forefront) promote a relationship that is based on "instinctive" and "chemical" attraction and the desire for those who are "hot" and "tough guys," facilitating rejection, indifference, and mistreatment. This has led me to reflect on the the key question of attraction. In relation to the other great concern, choice, I have provided an alternative approach after examining the main theories on this topic. Using this approach, I can specify the theories and practices necessary for the development of satisfactory sexual-affective relationships.

With regard to *attraction*, it is clear that love is a historical and social institution that we experience in a personal way. Thus, interpretations of love that involve instinct, "chemistry," or similar concepts have significant consequences. When the reason behind a phenomenon is unknown or the aim is to justify certain behavior with regard to attraction, we tend to search for biological, superstitious, or magical causes. Sociological, psychological, and anthropological explanations refer to attraction as an unstoppable lightning strike. Rather than evoking the magical origins of the lightning bolt as the anger of the gods, we should deeply examine the roots of attraction.

I demonstrate that if events do not occur in a "spontaneous" manner, then it is possible to avoid the "inevitable." Attraction is presented as a natural phenomenon that causes us to fall in love with women who are considered beautiful and men who represent strength and have more power than others. Considering that kindness (as synonymous with weakness) is associated with boredom and a lack of attractiveness, we arrive at the current social equation that stability and passion are irreconcilable. However, the research presented here demonstrates that the solution does not involve the search for stability in good people and passion in "attractive" people but in uniting the two concepts.

In the personal, social, and educational fields, this involves introducing and debating the subject by linking values to a type of person to reveal the connection between attraction and negative values and a lack of interest and positive values. These debates lead us to look for stability and excitement as well as sweetness and passion in the same person. They may also allow us to change our tastes, resocialize ourselves through dialogue and debates, and fall in love with people who have progressive values. A critical attitude toward the influence of the media, friends, and other socializing agents as well as the internalization of values around which consensus has been reached through debates will bring about everything that later "comes from so deep inside that we cannot avoid it."

Choice is always vital, particularly if we have not resolved *attraction* in a favorable manner. According to my analysis, choosing can be accomplished only communicatively or intersubjectively. This is the only type of choice that is not instrumental and that fits with dialogic learning, the basis of our educational model. Our final recommendation is to deliberately incorporate the significance of emotions into intersubjective choice. Egalitarian dialogue requires control over emotions because of the irrational weight that has been attached to them.

The primary aim is to define a new alternative model of sexual-affective relationships which promotes more satisfactory attractions and choices. This model is the conclusion of the twofold change, which also impacts communication. I carefully examined the traditional model and demonstrated that we have historically been relating to each other according to a conservative model, as though the loss of passion when combined with friendship or an increase in excitement when faced with bad treatment are biological changes that cannot be overcome. Stability and excitement as well as friendship and passion were not unlikely pairs. However, I have chosen a path that opens the door to love between equals, provides the opportunity to find affection and passion in the same person, and indicates that passion is not incompatible with equality. The new alternative model is based on the following characteristics of dialogic learning.

1. egalitarian dialogue, interpreting and organizing affective relationships based on dialogue and consensus without allowing oneself to be controlled by "irresistible" personal emotions or imposed power;
2. cultural intelligence – that is, all individuals have competences that involve different types of intelligence, skills and abilities that are linked to language and action;
3. transformation, as horizontal relationships have large transformative effects;
4. instrumental dimension, as we must understand how the social influences the personal, how and why we fall in love, who we fall in love with, what the environmental influences are, how we internalize these influences, and what the mechanisms that come into play are;
5. creation of meaning, dreams, and feelings that give meaning to life. Through equal communication that involves decisions concerning what will be discussed, in what way, when, and so on, creative abilities are developed, leading to new meaning and hopes;
6. solidarity, as the response to socialization cannot be achieved on an individual basis. Rather, it is based on joint experiences and personal feelings and collective knowledge constructed through egalitarian dialogue; and

7. equality of difference, as all people are equal and different. All people have the same right – based on differences – to learn according to what they perceive to be necessary in their affective sexual life.

This model discards the traditional model's three typologies (womanizers, women who imitate the masculine model, and stable passionless couples). It unites friendship and passion as well as excitement and affection in the same person, although with very different applications depending on each person's freedom of choice. The question of whether we are guided by this new model or the traditional model led us to conduct the current research.

The research reported here collected the opinions of adolescents, analyzed two magazines, and clarified the position with regard to preferences, tastes, and desires. For example, statements such as "I like this hot guy"; "he has cheated on me three times but he attracts me"; "my ex left me three times but it looks like he wants to get back together, what should I do?"; and "we want to go out with these guys who look down on us" were frequent. To address these statements and questions, magazines provided "educational" advice ("don't be silly"; "just go for it"; "allow yourself to follow your instinct," etc.) and encouraged superficial dates, a lack of tenderness, and a mistaken idea of passion. The critical theories that guide the alternative model of sexual-affective relationships are more advanced than the advice of "gossip" magazines.

According to the daily life stories and communicative focus groups, jealousy and fights are inherent to sexual-affective relationships; we fall in love – without wanting to – with people who irresistibly attract us; love at first sight is inevitable; and those who reject us have sex appeal. The stories and groups demonstrated that difficulty results in love, but an easy conquest brings a loss of interest. We desire people who are "energetic," have "personality," have smooth techniques rather than genuine feelings, and are only interested in their own ends. In short, we desire people who embody the characteristics of the traditional model of sexual-affective relationships. Furthermore, we feel attraction and desire for those who have the most power (boys) and the most beauty (girls) and feel only friendship, affection, and tenderness for those who do not embody power (boys) or beauty (girls) but who have good values and represent a stable future. That is, we either suffer from "irrational" passionate love or accept the type of love that provides security and stability but involving the express sacrifice of passion.

Television, the cinema, the Internet, song lyrics, and other vehicles of communication and socialization were not the subjects of our research.

However, it is easy to examine whether the hero or the "good guy" in the film is sensitive, peaceful, tender, and passionate or a "tough guy" who is violent (always "for a reason") and passionate and whether he sweeps, mops, and changes diapers. Internet websites and chat rooms related to sexual-affective relationships as well as popular songs should not be ignored. For example, a song by David Bisbal (a Spanish singer popular among adolescents) contains the lyrics:

> lie to me, condemn me, chain me up, seduce me, make me yours until I die of pain, lie to me, punish me, drive me crazy (...) and although I know I'll never stop loving you, your love is like a vice that I cannot give up, and the truth is that you are hurting me, your kisses are thorns but I want to give myself to you. ...

Given that we internalize the messages of the traditional model, it is not surprising that the research results present a negative picture of the type of people who we fall in love with.

We also make choices in accordance with various traditional types. We use rational choice (usually after the failure of "irrational" love) when we seek a secure relationship, although it leads us to relinquish passion and our dreams. In some cases, we may also use normative choice by paying attention to our peer group. However, we usually make an "irrational" choice, in which the emotions rule, resulting in a destructive love that is impossible to avoid.

To understand the true depth of the problem, we consider the following passage by Ortega y Gasset (1999), who demonstrated extraordinary insight when examining who we choose.

> The girl falls in love thus with the rake before he carries out any of his rakishness. Shortly afterwards, the husband pawns her jewels and leaves her. The female friends console the little lady without luck for her "mistake"; but in the deepest part of her conscience, she knows very well that there was not one, that she felt a suspicion of such possibilities from the beginning, and that this suspicion was an ingredient of her love, it was what "tasted" the best to her in that man. (Ortega y Gasset, 1999: 161)

It is interesting that during the early 20th century, rejection and deception were described as "tasting" the best. Can we say that issues in this area have substantially changed?

The transformative perspective of rational, passionate, reflexive, and emotional love, constructed through dialogue and the interaction of the two people in the relationship, allows us to freely decide who we fall in love with and who we reject and how to carry on the relationship and when and how to end it. The issues of attraction and choice require a profound global transformation in methodologies and types of learning, school models, and a full analysis of the underlying processes.

In other words, certain basic competencies must be incorporated into the sexual-affective domain (with the education system at the forefront) and a community model that allows us to identify the problems of attraction and solve them must be created. We must also determine the guidelines for choice and how to carry them out. Furthermore, we must deeply examine the reasons behind choice (tastes, preferences, desires, etc.) and how to transform it while at the same time leading the way toward a good choice within the framework of egalitarian relationships. The new communicative perspective in current dialogic societies, the communicative methodology, and the egalitarian participation of the entire educational community must be guaranteed to develop certain basic competencies necessary in the sexual-affective terrain.

Future prospects: The educational model and basic sexual-affective competencies

Despite the great influence of the coeducational philosophy and its impact on sexual-affective relationships, extensive institutional documentation, recommended texts and educational practices have revealed several far-reaching gaps that must be filled if people are to achieve satisfactory sexual-affective relationships:

- The coeducational philosophy has only recently incorporated the communicative approach and dialogic learning into its practices, making the transformation of the context difficult. (In this case, the context is the environment that surrounds sexual-affective relationships.) Nevertheless, it has begun to move in this direction, for example, through the contributions of dialogic feminism (Beck-Gernsheim, Butler & Puigvert, 2001).
- In the educational terrain, actions tend to be focused on boys and girls, the teachers, and the school itself. However, my current thesis is based on the educational community as a transformative subject. Thus, families, for example, should be incorporated into coeducational school planning and participate in talks, conferences, courses, debates, focus

groups or literary gatherings and should do so in an egalitarian manner. Thus, we demand the type of community school exemplified by the Schools as Learning Communities model among others.

- Equality in relationships is sought but without an in-depth consideration of the key questions of attraction or good choices as the basis of satisfactory sexual-affective relationships. Progress has been made in areas such as overcoming hierarchies, gender differences, the distance between the public-private lives of men and women, sexist language, texts and material, and so on; however, this progress has not reached the core of our problem. For example, although violence in relationships is harshly criticized, its depths are not probed unless we deal with the eradication of certain values that are related to attraction.

An in-depth examination of the acquisition of competencies related to attraction, choice, and equality is unavoidable. These competencies should be interrelated as we consider how to approach the model, the methodology, and perspective on which it is based. We wish to successfully respond to questions such as the following: What basic sexual-affective competences should be acquired? How can satisfactory sexual-affective relationships be developed over a lifetime? What conditions are required to access these competencies? Are there perspectives that are more facilitative? What is the best methodology? What is the best school model?

Educational model

If we view increased learning, decreased coexistence problems, participation by the whole educational community, and solidarity as indicators of success, then the international scientific community has many successful programs and projects.[1] These schools open their doors to members of the community and are transformed while providing an egalitarian response to the challenges of the contemporary society.

The model's basis is that all children have a right to an education that will allow them to develop satisfactory sexual-affective relationships and that does not condemn them to a problematic relationship as a precursor to an unsatisfactory life. To provide such education, schools must be governed by an egalitarian model of society and propose a type of learning that is in accordance with new social structures (dialogic learning). This will change not only student learning but also the organization of the school and the environment, down to the individual classroom. Thus, the following elements are significant: participation of all educational agents, a focus on learning so that all individuals develop their abilities at the maximum level, high expectations (for the students and for all people who collaborate in the educational process), promotion of individual abilities, and constant assessment that guarantees permanent progress.

We focus on participation, an essential element that allows community resources to be optimized through planning and joint action. All people involved contribute their own initiatives, suggestions for improvement, knowledge, and know-how to the project. Because people have different life-worlds, this method provides a great deal of richness. We must determine the type of sexual-affective relationship that we want to put into practice. The current proposal is based on the alternative model and can be incorporated into the debate on the type of sexual-affective relationship desired and the search for a result that derives from dialogue and consensus in the maximum number of fields possible. Debaters include school professionals, educators, social workers, leisure center workers, family members, students, associations, companies, and city councils, among others. We are talking about dreaming freely about those relationships that one desires to have, because we have to add a complement to scientific value: illusion, utopias. And with them, the three aspects that give them life:

- High expectations. We can achieve certain basic competencies that will facilitate a very satisfactory affective and sexual life.
- Dreams. We will not achieve our goals if dreams are missing. Science should be conceived with dreams.
- The feeling that we can transform reality. Although we believe that sexual-affective relationships are difficult, that we drag serious family burdens behind us, that we coexist with physical, mental, and sexual violence, and that we do not know what to do when certain situations arise, we must believe that we are capable of changing everything.

The guideline on which these points are based – that the sexual-affective relationships that we wish for our children and friends should be the same that we wish for every girl and every boy – not only avoids a double discourse but also generates shared elements, thus preventing sexual-affective failure. It is important to ensure that all educational agents (family members, members of the administration, teachers, students, etc.) share this objective. Here, the challenge will be to achieve consensus through dialogue on crucial subjects such as attraction, choice, and equality.

For example, debates and talks on issues linked to this subject with boys and girls of various ages can be held within these spaces. Family members and people from the community can be involved in these debates. From such debates, new dreams can be derived, including various activities that involve a discussion of sexual-affective relationships:

- Film nights. A mixed committee can organize film nights, select the films, and make the resources available. The debate encouraged following the films should tackle the subjects of attraction, choice, equality, and the impact of such types of films. The debate must also be based on dialogic learning, placing an emphasis on the principle of egalitarian dialogue, to ensure that the participation of the maximum number of people provides richness and new elements for change and reflection.
- Training centers that provide classes for family members, teachers, and other social agents (especially families, given their significant impact). Another committee selected from the above groups could organize these classes, obtain resources, plan the program, and demonstrate the specific approach so that the necessary interaction can be generated to deeply delve into these subjects.
- A forum for debate on the Internet. A committee (again composed of various educational and social agents) could also organize this forum, suggest subjects for debate, and redirect when appropriate. The committee could respond to the contributions and questions, keeping the forum active.

However, who should or can move these activities forward? If we focus school organization on one figure (as tends to happen), it is unlikely that we will achieve these dreams. Work groups will allow these transformations to be carried out, as each group will take on the responsibility of ensuring that each objective is achieved.

If we begin with the idea that learning and the development of skills and competencies (in the current case, attraction, choice, and equality) increasingly depend on dialogue and interaction, we must guarantee that the work on these subjects is carried out through the greatest amount of rich interaction possible. In addition, it requires egalitarian dialogue, which eliminates the impositions made through force and replaces them with powerful arguments.

If learning in heterogeneous and interactive groups generates grassroots solidarity, the desired competencies will be constructed by all participants rather than be imposed upon them. Incorporating family members and/or volunteers to motivate and tutor each activity group promotes an in-depth debate. For example, if we divide a group of twenty students into four heterogeneous groups using the criteria specified, they can work on different activities (with the help of another adult). These activities may include, for example, verbal commentary on a video, reading part of the text in a magazine that addresses the subject of interest, writing comments on the text, or contributing to an Internet forum that is shared with other schools in the region.

Designing spaces in the curriculum to work on sexual-affective relationships while maintaining traditional timetables and spaces without accounting for the aspects addressed in these talks or debate will either lead girls and boys to not take the work on sexual-affective relationships seriously or make them perceive it to be a subject that is remote from their daily lives. The active participation of the whole community, especially students, family members, and other adults from the educational context, can contribute to a consensus by incorporating their various lifeworlds into the curriculum.

It is necessary to make the aspects related to sexual-affective relationships an integral part of the curriculum in order to minimize the possibility of them being ignored or cast aside. Therefore, students would not only learn about their own gender roles and how to both assume and operate under authority (the most valued and significant cultural knowledge) but also why certain girls and boys are liked and others are not and how to choose better partners, and so on. Making all this explicit indicates that the community as a whole can decide how, when, and in what way to address these subjects in the school.

Basic competencies

The key concept is love. We follow Giddens (1993) here, who considers love a consequence of modernity and the freedom dynamic that it generates, experiencing the ideals of romantic love and the emergence of sexuality as characteristic of modernity. Thus, we understand love to be a natural part of the human experience that is found in all societies and is closely connected to marriage.

We add Beck and Beck-Gernsheim's (1995) definition to that of Giddens. The former viewed contemporary love as a phenomenon that must be constructed and a never-ending shared project. "Love under modern conditions is not an event which takes place once but is a state to be fought for anew every day" (Beck and Beck-Gernsheim, 1995: 99).

To this type of love, a relationship that must be cultivated daily, we add all the feelings that one person has for another as manifested through the desire for that person's company and through joy about what is good and distress about what is bad for that person. With that in mind, mistreatment, violence, indifference, and rejection are unmistakable signs of a lack of love. The basic competencies will identify such actions as exclusionary sexual-affective dimensions and, consequently, reject sexual-affective relationships based on these dimensions.

Certain conditions must be encouraged to properly acquire these competencies:

- Solidarity. The groups are established in an interactive manner, resulting in diverse characteristics (social class, gender, age, ethnic origin, and educational level), and involve teamwork based on solidarity.
- Multiculturalism. Multiculturalism is both a fact and a benefit. It involves being united in diversity and respecting the equality of differences.
- Coherence. Words should correspond to facts. Reason should not be remote from the emotions, which, in turn, should not contradict reason. Desires that contradict solid arguments must be reconstructed.
- Knowledge. Knowledge, rather than superstition, myths, or magic, must serve as the basis for analysis. We do not believe that love is biological or impulsive but is based on historical and socially imposed sexual-affective relationships.
- Choice of method. We indicate various methods, depending on the subjects and potential sources for data collection; however, in general, we recommend communicative focus groups or dialogic gatherings. For example, we recommend periodic meetings at which each person underlines what is most important to him/her in the subject under discussion. These responses are then presented, discussed, and, thus, enrich the whole group. The group then gathers together the contributions, which are based on valid arguments.

Rather than conducting an exhaustive study of all competencies, I divided them into attraction-related, choice-related, and equality-related. Students, teachers, and the whole educational community can develop.

Attraction-related competencies

1. *Developing love as a feeling with a social origin rather than a spontaneous origin.* This requires an understanding that love is not instinctive or impulsive, does not occur in an inevitable manner, and does not strike like a bolt of lightning. Although love may seem spontaneous, it is not. This competency involves attacking the "irrational" aspect of love and endorsing love as historical and social.

   Topics: The symbols of women (the mirror of beauty) and of men (the lance and the shield) date from the distant past. An examination of their meaning confirms how canons of beauty have been transformed over time, paying attention to cultural changes and verifying the physical types that are promoted through magazines, TV series, and films so each reader or viewer feels attracted to them on an individual level as if it were a "personal" attraction, "chemistry," and what "comes from inside."

   Methodology: Students should watch TV series or films, followed by a general debate in a class or various classes, depending on the type of series or film and the school resources. Students can read and discuss books and magazines in small, interactive groups and later move into a debate in a large group. In other words, we use communicative methodology on interactive groups and large-group discussion to reach agreements, even if they are minimal. At least on occasion, educational agents should also participate in the discussion on a level equal to that of the students. These agents can include teachers, family members, social workers, educators, and representatives of the administration and institutions, etc.

2. *Critically examining the media as the creators of a type of love based on the traditional model.* This competency ensures that all students become critical of the traditional model and then are able to reject it. It involves observation and the subsequent analysis of the values that the media indicate as attractive. It is especially important to underline aspects such as a lack of respect, violence, "irrationality," sexism and whatever stereotypes remain – "tough" guys and "good" girls, "smart" guys and "easy" girls, etc.

   Topics: An examination of how the media convey a lack of respect in boy–girl relationships and how the media treat violence of all types and promote and justify violent people. It is also necessary to analyze what is attractive about the "tough" guys and the "hot girls" and how they are promoted as well as why "smart" guys have their own way but "easy girls" are punished. Such an analysis could also be conducted on other instances of sexism and stereotypes. There are many available examples of the most sought-after girls and boys in advice pages in magazines, song lyrics, heroes and heroines in all media, and so on.

Methodology: Depending on the method of communication and the topic, students can watch films and hold subsequent large-group debates. Or magazines and/or newspapers can be read in small, interactive groups or a debate on song lyrics can be held in a large group. In short, the values of the people who are "recommended to us" can be compared to the values derived from the alternative model. This employs the communicative methodology and, when possible, the horizontal participation of the various educational agents.

3. *Rejecting the people who act in opposition to the alternative model* – those who look down on others, use any type of violence, use people as objects, etc. This involves adopting a critical position in relation to many of the most sought-after people in the media. This competency represents the first step toward a personal change because it involves rejecting attractive people who have negative values.

Topics: All of the love stories and sexual-affective relationships in which one of the protagonists plays a role that involves lack of respect, putting people down, violence, and so on. If it is not suitable to discuss a real-life situation for reasons of discretion, privacy, etc., videos, films, and television series can easily be used for this topic. Interesting paragraphs in many novels and love stories can be underlined for group discussion. The group can choose those examples that it finds most interesting.

Methodology: Advice columns in magazines or love stories in books can be analyzed in search of passages that describe rejection and gender violence. This methodology also provides an opportunity to present communicative daily life stories in which some of the participants offer an actual case to the group. This case is then analyzed, either in a large group or in small, interactive groups. If the group knows of any such relationships, then communicative focus groups can be undertaken. Communicative observations are not feasible unless they involve cooperation and both parties have knowledge of the observation.

4. *Attraction to people who develop the values based on the alternative model–* those who understand the importance of friendship, good treatment, affection, appreciation of, and concern for others and base their relationships on sincerity, equality, and deep feelings. This competency represents the second step in achieving a personal change in desires. It involves rejecting those who only pretend to be in love while feeling an attraction to those who truly love.

Topics: Those related to relationships and stories of people who love each other, treat each other well, and desire each other. The short bibliography and filmography that exist on this subject should be collected, as it is difficult to find examples based on the alternative model. However, we always have examples in our friends for re-evaluation. The group becomes the agent of change in tastes, desires, preferences, and attraction.

Methodology: In this case, it is important to carry out a communicative observation of the sexual-affective relationships that are based on equality and sincere feelings. The joint data collection can enrich the subsequent group debate. A case study of a relationship that serves as a role model for "good practices" in the affective sexual field can be performed.

5. *Uniting in the same person feelings of passion and friendship, madness and affection, while rejecting people who represent the traditional model.* This overcomes the traditional problem of attraction – the duality between passion or madness and friendship or affection. To date, passion has been inspired by the powerful and the most beautiful. On the other hand, friendship is linked to "good" people in such a way that friendship and passion do not seem to be found for the same person. The competency presented here creates a union between the good guy and the sexy guy as well as between the good woman and the sexy woman. We demonstrate that what is considered sexy is socially influenced and thus able to be changed.

Topics: The link between being a good person and a friend as well as the traditional association between not being attractive and an object of passion. In general, this topic investigates which values imply attractiveness, which do not, and the reasons why. For example, if a successful concert is given by a man, is he viewed as attractive even though he is not good-looking? On the other hand, if the musician is a woman, is she only viewed as attractive if she is good-looking? We must also be sure to examine the relationships (even if they are scarce) in which both affection and passion occur at the same time in two people.

Methodology: This competency can be examined through case studies of people who represent the paradigm of good values, always being a good friend, and never being viewed as attractive. (Case studies of people who are viewed as attractive and have certain negative values can be performed at the same time.) We also recommend a communicative daily life story in which this situation is described. Cases in which love is created and in which both stability and passion are evident in both members of a couple must be examined and discussed.

Choice-related competencies

1. *Understanding, distinguishing, and choosing among the different types of choice, prioritizing the intersubjective.* It is important to acknowledge (1) rational choice, (2) choice based on social norms (3) choice that is dependent on emotions, and (4) choice through intersubjectivity.

   Topics: The topics coincide with the four types of choice. Specifically, the topics include choosing according to a purpose (searching for stability, a good social position, a good reputation, etc.), according to social norms (choosing people who the peer group considers to be attractive or who the family approves, etc.), allowing oneself to be carried away with emotion (those who, although they fear the worst, are swept along or those who attract by being theatrical – for example, pretending that they like a person when they do not) – and choosing in an intersubjective manner (discussing in depth the reasons behind feelings and previous relationships, etc.). Films, books or magazines as well as real stories can be selected. This competency can be used to clarify the different methods of choosing relationships, the reasons behind them, and their consequences.

   Methodology: similar to the first competency on attraction (developing love as a feeling with a social origin rather than as an instinct or an impulse), we prioritize intersubjectivity. Therefore, TV series or films can be selected for a viewing that involves a general debate, depending on the type of series or film chosen. In the case of magazines or books, the various choices can be examined and discussed in small, interactive groups, followed by a large-group debate. We continue to use the communicative methodology through interactive groups and debates in a large group in the form of a literary gathering for the best results. As many educational agents as possible should participate, including students, teachers, family members, educators, social workers, leisure center instructors, representatives of administrations and institutions, and so on.

2. *Being aware of validity claims and taking them into account when choosing.* Habermas's (1987a, 1987b) theory inspires us, and this competency helps us to choose based on scientific criteria (the truth) and morals (according to the alternative model) while, at the same time, allowing us freedom in regard to aesthetics (each person has his/her own taste in beauty). Because in other instances we look to science rather than superstition, we use the "true or false" criteria, providing arguments with the intention of universally convincing.

In the field of morality, we use arguments that are also based on the criteria of "good or bad," as we do not consider everything to be relative. On the other hand, with regard to aesthetics, we use the criterion of "pretty or ugly," as we are aware that, although social pressure plays a large role, all individuals have their own tastes. Therefore, we do not need to reach a consensus on or convince other people to change their beauty-related criteria.

Topics: The topics and examples to be discussed in groups are suggested in the paragraphs above. One subject is the scientific basis when choosing, another is the moral basis, and a third (especially important) basis is desire, which tends to prevail over the other criteria.

Methodology: This competency requires the analysis of books and magazines that portray different options, both scientific and moral, and their repercussions when making choices in sexual-affective relationships. To contrast the texts with contexts, it is advisable to analyze real situations through communicative focus groups. Such debates are enriched when it is demonstrated that not everyone behaves in the same way. Discussion participants make clear a relationship based on love is different than one than one based on imminent rejection, and their consequences are different. It is crucial to demonstrate that if desire is the driving force behind our acts, then such desire must be based on scientific and moral criteria.

3. *Identifying and eliminating situations in which desire is opposed to reason.* I prioritize argumentation. If the best argument contradicts desire and if consensus is opposed to this attraction, then the situation must

be resolved by prioritizing argumentation. This competency requires the commitment to pay attention to the group when desire and reason are viewed as opposites. The idea of reaching agreements to fulfill them later is promoted. This must be addressed in depth, as it is difficult to hold back desire when it is strong, despite a commitment to do so.

Topics: Although the subject is unique (desire vs. reason), the examples are varied and can be inspired by cases of "obsession," such as "I would have done anything he or she said"; "she/he lost his head over him/her"; "he/she seemed like another person"; "there was no way to reason with him/her"; "she/he ended up giving up everything for him/her"; "he/she was destroyed and then ended up alone," and so on.

Methodology: This subject can be analyzed through books, magazines, and so on. It can also be discussed in life stories that describe the "craziness" of love. Films can be analyzed through communicative focus groups prior to analysis in a larger group. Case studies can also be useful. All activities should be immersed in the communicative perspective and its principles.

4. *Becoming aware that choice is only correct if it is in agreement with the values of the alternative model.* The different types of choice, assumptions of validity, and the false conflict between desire and reason are examined. Then this section is completed by emphasizing that the only choice that can guarantee satisfactory relationships is made according to the definition of love. This competence can be used to evaluate sexual-affective relationships based on what these relationships mean and how the people in the relationship treat each other.

Topics: the relationships that are most in accordance with the definition of love. An additional topic is the importance that boys and girls place on the stipulation that their partners do not have other relationships (and the reasons why). Furthermore, relationships should be analyzed exclusively in relation to people's behavior and how the people involved in the relationship treat each other. Finally, jealousy and envy must be investigated. Do we invest more of our time, concern, thoughts, and desires into what our partners are doing or stop doing, who they are meeting or who they are thinking about than into constructing together a relationship that is based on love?

Methodology: a group debate in communicative focus groups when the subject is rather theoretical and either addresses relationships based

on the alternative model or the reasons why we do not want our partners to have other relationships. In examining jealousy and envy, the
subject of violence is quite significant. It is advisable to analyze specific cases (in the press and documentary reports) of extreme situations. When we wish to analyze what occurs in couples, in addition
to communicative focus groups, we can use techniques such as communicative observation for cases in which couples are in agreement.
This material is quite rich (especially with regards to jealousy) because
it is addressed in the most celebrated works of universal literature and
the most famous films. Thus, this examination can be an excellent
opportunity to unite learning about relationships with expanding our
knowledge of literature and art.

Equality-related competencies

We do not extensively discuss this section because, although attraction and
choice (especially the former) have not been addressed in depth, equality has
been the subject of significant study. Furthermore, educational proposals that
involve material and activities, especially in the area of coeducation, exist.
However, we can provide an innovative perspective, with the aim of enriching the debate and the proposals themselves.

1. *Being aware of power hierarchies and the way in which we internalize them
   from birth.* Fathers, mothers, teachers, policemen, and policewomen
   represent positions of superiority that people must submit to. We learn
   to achieve positions of power and therefore internalize both the idea
   of obeying and the notion of giving people orders. In its most extreme
   manifestation, we internalize slavery and dictatorship. This competency can be used to position ourselves in the world and reflect on how
   we take part in it, even in its aspects that we criticize.
   Topics: We can choose the examples that most attract our attention
   from among the various power-related relationships. It is useful to analyze examples that involve parents, family members, and teachers. The
   difficulty lies in demonstrating the power claims of all of the people
   involved, the step that precedes overcoming power relations.
   Methodology: Communicative focus groups are recommended here
   because all people are involved in this subject, which is experienced
   daily. Once again, the active and egalitarian participation of families
   and teachers is important. This is an important opportunity to establish

common criteria and promote egalitarian dialogue among the various educational agents.

2. *Developing a critical spirit in relation to the patriarchy and the various fundamentalisms.* It is important to understand the way in which the patriarchy has evolved, the aims and reasons behind current fundamentalisms, and the various feminist perspectives and how they are differentiated. This competency explains gender relationships and helps to move them toward an egalitarian perspective.

   Topics: among others, cases of extreme patriarchy and religious fundamentalism (such as the Taliban regime), which aim to justify a return to the past as a defense against invasive Western society (as has been the case of Algeria). In addition, Western religious fundamentalism, which opposes the use of condoms, for example, can be examined. The feminism of equality, the feminism of difference, and the feminism of the equality of difference are also included amongst these topics.

   Methodology: Data analysis is needed in relation to questions of extreme patriarchy and religious fundamentalism. General debates can be held following the communicative focus groups generated as a result of the data analysis. For a debate on different forms of feminism, films and the abundant literature on this subject can be studied. The participation of the whole educational community becomes especially interesting in this case. Interesting exchanges of opinion concerning the forced use of the veil, its prohibition, or women's freedom of choice can be carried out.

3. *Developing sexual-affective relationships based on equality rather than power: solidarity and friendship as the generators of love and passion.* In a capitalist globalized world (lacking solidarity in itself), the development of other relationships that promote equality is important. This competency generates new expectations of transformative identities and, therefore, stimulates opportunities to establish satisfactory sexual-affective relationships based on equality. In some ways, this competency facilitates falling in love with friends – falling in love with people who have excellent values and who we have connected with affection but never with passion.

   Topics: Examples of relationships that involve strong elements of solidarity, friendship, love, and passion. These egalitarian and generous relationships can be compared with the traditional model of power relations and relationships based on stability but lack passion. Through this comparison, within the framework of equality, we can differentiate between stable friendships without passion and stable friendships filled with passion as we plan future relationships.

Methodology: When stable relationships with no passion or power relations are examined, communicative daily life stories or data analysis (many magazines and films provide relevant information) can be employed, although the final objective is to facilitate a large-group debate. However, when discussing plans for the future, it is best to hold debates in communicative focus groups.

A final note: Whenever possible, we recommend the use of Internet debate forums concerning these three competencies. This is an additional means of enriching and promoting participation.

In short, in this book, I demonstrate that we are attracted to and choose our partners based on the traditional model of sexual-affective relationships. We also discover that we need an alternative model that should be developed daily and serve as a guide to attraction and choice. Furthermore, we specify some basic competencies that should be acquired in relation to attraction, choice, and equality. These competencies will aid in putting the new model into practice. Finally, all these aspects are included within the framework of a community educational model. Thus, by changing our tastes, desires, and preferences, we will be able to choose according to what we have internalized in the same way that, through good communication, we can end superficial fights and discuss our feelings, thoughts, desires, and fantasies in depth.

This is the way we can achieve love between equals that is motivating and not boring, achieve profound social transformations accompanied by personal transformations, and obtain scientific knowledge about love and the socialization that accompanies it. It is also how we can realize the dream of uniting passion and affection as well as stability and excitement at the same time, over the long term, and with the same person. In short, we can construct sexual-affective relationships that will continue to be exciting and moving with the people who truly love us and unite passion and equality, friendship and excitement, stability and desire.

In some ways, we incorporate arguments and transformations that can aid in resolving the old dilemma in the affective-sexual field between Marxists and Weberians concerning the predominance of the infrastructure or the super-structure. Marx (1970) defended the superiority of the infrastructure (the social being determines consciousness). However, when seeking the link between Protestant ethics and the development of capitalism, Weber (1999) aimed to do the opposite. Do we do what our consciousness tells us (Weber), or do we do what we wish and then search for arguments to justify it (Marx)? If we acquire the basic competencies that allow us to establish satisfactory sexual -affective relationships, then we can nearly eliminate this contradiction, as we view the two concepts as coinciding.

I am aware that reproduction, relativism, the traditional model, and the strength of socializing agents are powerful enemies. However, I also believe in the strength of reason and feelings. Therefore, in line with Freire (1997), I embrace the notion of transforming difficulties into possibilities, because we are not animals but beings of transformation rather than adaptation.

AFTERWORD

Lídia Puigvert

The memory of Pato singing passionately for radical love and the glow in his eyes when he was together with Joe Kincheloe and Paulo Freire is part of the legacy of this work.[1] We can see within this book and also in the conversations he had with scholars like Paulo and Joe not only their shared commitment to make this world a better place than the one they had found but also the evidence that they actually accomplished this.

These are just two of the voices that remind us of this fact:

> Pato changed my life (…). The day I met him, he started to fill my professional life with joy, light and meaning… and he helped me so much in my personal life as well. (Marcos, member of "Men in Dialogue")

> Reading this book was revealing to me, because it made me believe in and want to desire radical love forever. Since then, every time I read it again, together with the many stories that friends had told me about Pato, make me feel lucky because, even without knowing him, I feel like having radically transformative conversations with him…conversations with Pato through his words full of passion, feelings, and rigor. (Emilia, doctoral student)

For years we worked together on the theories on love he was developing and the feminist theories some of us were analyzing. From his first contribution and our joint work, our colleagues have unravelled concepts and analyses he had initially introduced in this book, such as: a) how to identify crucial aspects in the socialization of youth and adolescents (i.e., the mirage of upward mobility and romantic love[2]); b) how to transform desire (i.e., language of desire – language of ethics[3]); c) how to choose well (i.e., new masculinities[4]); and d) how to create spaces of Zero violence since the age of Zero (i.e., the dialogic model of conflict prevention and response[5]).

Contributing scientific knowledge to such an unexplored field brought great enthusiasm for Pato but also attacks and defamations from those who felt that their power and areas of influence were being questioned. Resistance arose from colleagues – and persons who were not so collegial who read into his words both an overwhelming theoretical approach and a brave and coherent behaviour that questioned the foundations of gender violence. Despite the attempts to destroy him, his unconditional support of and solidarity with these shared ideas has instead made his work much more valuable and attractive.

We are many – the scholars, educators and youth who want to continue building on the arenas that Pato initiated, exploring forms and theories yet to be imagined. The translation into English of this work will, no doubt, extend this reality.

His most precious legacies: that we dare to make his dream – the revolution of the 21st century – become real; the life of his son enjoying tenderness and passion in his relationship; and the dream of a better world for Ainara, his daughter. In the book that Ramon wrote for his god daughter, we find these words: "You will hear about him in all parts of the world, and people who never met him will debate about his main contribution: his theory of love (…). Even if you don't say a word, a smile will spring up from deep inside, because you will already know that he left with such plenitude from what he considered his greatest legacy: the love with Lidia from which you were born, and the joy with which he kissed you and caressed you when you were still in your mother's belly."

As a result of all this, there comes a new dream, Ainara's dream: "Friendship is only to be with our friends, and not to mistake them for others who are not good and who are not intelligent" (Ainara, 7 years old).

NOTES

Introduction

1. We collected information from a popular magazine for young people (*Ragazza*) and contrasted it with information from a magazine for adults (*Cosmopolitan*). We also gathered information from sixteen communicative daily life stories and four communicative focus groups.

Chapter 1

1. These include a psychoanalysis (Freud, 1975) in which repression and the unconscious play a fundamental role, symbolic interactionism (Mead, 1990) with the "generalised other," and cognitive development (Piaget, 1968), for which its stages serve as the universal features of socialization.
2. Spanish saying "Quien bien te quiere te hará llorar."
3. Building upon Gomez's research, later studies (Flecha, Puigvert, and Ríos, 2013) have differentiated between two types of traditional masculinities: dominant traditional masculinity (DTM) and oppressed traditional masculinity (OTM). In this book, however, the traditional model of masculinity refers, most of the time, to dominant traditional masculinity (DTM).
4. "I thank thee from the bottom of my heart for the desperation you cause me, and I detest the tranquility in which I lived before knowing thee. I clearly see what the remedy would

be for all for my ills, and I would feel free from them if I stopped loving thee. But, it cannot be helped! No, I prefer to suffer than to forget thee. Oh! Does this perchance depend on me? I cannot reproach myself for having wanted to not love thee just for one instant, and when all is said and done thou art more worthy of compassion, and it is better to suffer everything I suffer than to enjoy the most languid pleasures which are supplied to thee by thy lovers in France." *The first letter ends thus*: "Goodbye, love me always and make me suffer even greater ills" (Ortega y Gasset, 1999: 68). [My translation].

Chapter 2

1. Since the time of Aristotle, teleological action has been the central point of the theory of action. The actor achieves an end or produces the desired state of things by choosing the most coherent means in a given situation and applying it in a suitable manner (Habermas, 1987a: 122).

Chapter 3

1. In the United States either *mixed-sex/gender education* or *coeducation* is used. In Spain, *Mixed schools* are not the same as *coeducational schools*: *Mixed schools* came just after Franco's dictatorship. Placing boys and girls together within the schools' classrooms was mandatory but inequalities persisted and were not questioned. Some years later, accepting that the *Mixed schools* were not enough to end with inequalities among sexes, schools were asked to move to *coeducation*, which means not only joining both sexes together but also questioning gender inequalities.

2. There are other definitions; Ortega y Gasset (1999) used the word "calavera" [literally "skull," or metaphorically, a man with poor judgement], although perhaps "womanizers" or "playboys" are the most commonly used translations. Throughout this book, the term "womanizers," as used by Giddens, is employed.

3. The cover text of *Ragazza* for February 2004 reflects this notion: "Extra AMOR. Test ¿Eres dulce o apasionada?" [LOVE supplement. Test: Are you sweet or passionate?]

4. An ideal type of school includes the "Learning Communities" model.

Chapter 4

1. Here, I reference Western societies, although I have found no evidence that the questions of attraction and choice differ in other societies.

2. Here, I refer to the contributions made by phenomenology (Schütz and Luckmann, 1977), constructivism (Berger and Luckmann, 1968), interactionism (Mead, 1990), ethnomethodology (Garfinkel, 1986), dramaturgy (Goffman, 1981), and, more recently, communicative action (Habermas, 1987a and 1987b), dialogic action (Freire, 1970 and 1997b), dialogic learning (Flecha, 1997), and the Risk Society (Beck, 1998a and 2000).

3. From now on, R refers to researcher and P refers to participant, and the number attached to P differentiates individual participants. Later, G will refer to participants in the communicative focus groups.
4. G refers to participants in the focus groups.

Chapter 5

1. To examine the subject more deeply, it is advisable to consult Elboj et al. (2002), in which the Learning Communities project for transformation in schools and its theoretical basis are clearly and precisely described. The same model has been used successfully in adult education (Sánchez, 1999). Other examples include the School Development Program (Comer, Haynes, Joyner and Ben-Avie, 1996), Accelerated Schools (Levin, 1998), and Success for All (Slavin, 1989 and 1990), among others.

Afterword

1. Freireproject.org
2. Puigvert, L. (2014). Preventive socialization of gender violence: Moving forward using the communicative methodology of research. *Qualitative Inquiry*, September 2014 20: 839–843. June 16.
3. Flecha, A., Puigvert, L. (2010). Contributions to social theory from Dialogic Feminism: Giving voice to all women. In *Examining social theory: Crossing borders/reflecting back*, D. E. Chapman, ed. Pp. 161–174. New York; Peter Lang.
4. Flecha, R., Puigvert, L., & Ríos, O. (2013). The new alternative masculinities and the overcoming of gender violence. *International and Multidisciplinary Journal of Social Sciences*, 2 (1), 88–113.
5. Gómez, A., Munté, A., & Sordé, T. (2014). Transforming schools through minority males' participation: Overcoming cultural stereotypes and preventing violence. *Journal of Interpersonal Violence*. doi:10.1177/0886260513515949

REFERENCES

Ackerman, D. (1994). *A natural history of love*. London: Vintage Books.

Alberdi, I., and Martínez, L. (1988). *Guía didáctica para una orientación no sexista*. Madrid: MEC, Serie Coeducación.

Altable, C. (1998). *Penélope o las trampas del amor*. Valencia: Mare Nostrum.

Altable, C. (2000). *Educación sentimental y erótica para adolescentes*. Madrid: Miño y Dávila.

Apple, M. W. (1993). *Democratic education in a conservative Age*. New York: Routledge

Apple, M. W., and Beane, J. A. (1997). *Escuelas democráticas*. Madrid: Morata (v.o. 1995)

Aubert, A., and García, C. (2001). Interactividad en el aula. *Cuadernos de Pedagogía, 301*, 20–24.

Ayuste, A., Flecha, R., López, F., and Lleras, J. (1994). *Planteamientos de la pedagogía Crítica. Comunicar y Trasformar*. Barcelona: Graó.

Barragán, F. (1998). Las razones del corazón. Afectividad, sexualidad y currículo. *Cuadernos de Pedagogía, 271*, 72–76.

Barragán, F. (1999). *Programa de educación afectivo sexual. Educación secundaria I. Sexualidad, educación sexual y género*. Sevilla: Junta de Andalucía – Consejería de Educación y Ciencia e Instituto Andaluz de la Mujer.

Bartolomé, M. (1992). Investigaciones cualitativa en educación: ¿Comprender o trasformar? *Revista de Investigación Educativa, 20*, 7–36.

Bartolomé, M. (Coord.) (1997). *Evaluación de un programa de educación intercultural: desarrollo de la identidad étnica en secundaria a través de la acción tutorial*. Informe final de investigación presentado al CIDE. Documento policopiado.

Bartolomé, M. (Coord.) (2002). *Identidad y ciudadanía: un reto a la educación intercultural*. Madrid: Narcea.

Bartolomé, M., Cabrera, F., Del Campo, J., Espín, J. V., Marín, M. A., Rodríguez, M., Sandín, M. P., and Sabariego, M. (2001a). *La construcción de la identidad en contextos multiculturales*. Madrid: CIDE.

Bartolomé, M., Cabrera, F., Del Campo, J., Espín, J. V., Marín, M. A., Rodríguez, M., Sandín, M. P., and Sabariego, M. (2001b). *La construcción de la identidad en contextos multiculturales*. Madrid: CIDE.

Bartolomé, M., Cabrera, F., Espín, J. V., Del Campo, J., Marín, M. A., Massot, I., Rodríguez, M., Sabariego, M., and Ávarez, E. M. (2001). *L 'Educació per a una Ciutadania Intercultural a Catalunya al 2° cicle d'ESO*. Informe de Investigación. Documento policopiado.

Beck, U. (1997). La reivindicación de la política: Hacia una teoría de la modernización reflexiva. En Beck, U., Giddens, A., and Lash, S., *Modernización reflexiva. Política, tradición y estética en el orden social moderno* (pp. 13–73). Madrid: Alianza (v.o. 1994).

Beck, U. (1998a). *La sociedad del riesgo*. Barcelona: Paidós (v.o. 1986).

Beck, U. (1998b). *¿Qué es la globalización?* Barcelona: Paidós (v.o. 1997).

Beck, U. (2000). *Un nuevo mundo feliz: la precariedad del trabajo en la era de la globalización*. Barcelona: Paidós (v.o. 1999).

Beck, U. (2002). *Libertad o capitalsmo*. Barcelona: Paidós (v.o. 2000).

Beck, U., and Beck-Gernsheim, E. (1995). *The normal chaos of Love*. Cambridge: Polity Press. (v.o. 1990).

Beck, U.; Giddens, A., and Lash, S. (1997). *Modernización reflexiva. Política tradición y estética en el orden social moderno*. Madrid: Alianza (v.o. 1994).

Beck-Gernsheim, E., Butler, J., y Puigvert, L. (2001). *Mujeres y trasformaciones sociales*. Barcelona: El Roure.

Benhabib, S. (1992). *Situating the self. Gender, community and postmodernism in contemporary ethics*. London: Polity Press.

Bercovich, L. (1996). *Seducción: ¿comunicación o engaño?* Buenos Aires: Nuevo Extremo.

Berger, P., and Luckmann, T. (1968). *La construcción social de la realidad*. Buenos Aires: Amorrortu (v.o. 1996).

Bernstein, B. (1988–1989). *Clases, códigos y control, Vols. I–II*. Madrid: Akal (v.o. 1971–1973).

Bernstein, B. (1990). *Poder, educación y conciencia*. Barcelona: El Roure.

Bernstein, B. (1993). *El discurso pedagógico*. Madrid: Morata (v.o. 1990).

Berscheid, E. (1993). Emotion. En Kelley, H. H., et al., *Close relationships* (pp. 110–168). New York: Freeman.

Berscheid, E., and Walster, E. (1974). Physical attractiveness. En Borkowitz, L. (Comp.), *Advances in experimental social psychology, Vol. 7* (pp. 157–215). New York: Academic Press.

Bloom, A. (1995). *El canon occidental*. Barcelona: Anagrama (v.o. 1994).

Blumstein, P., and Kollock, P. (1988). Personal relationships. *Annual Review of Sociology, 14*, 467–490.

Bonal, X. (1997). *Las actitudes del profesorado ante la coeducación. Propuestas de intervención*. Barcelona: Graó.

Bonal, X., and Rambla, X. (2001). El cambio ideológico y la colaboración docente. En Rambla, X., and Tomé, A. (Eds.), *Contra el sexismo. Coeducación y democracia en la escuela* (pp. 113–128). Madrid: Editorial Síntesis.

Bourdieu, P. (1988). *La distinción: Criterios y bases sociales del gusto*. Madrid: Taurus (v.o. 1979).

Bourdieu, P. (1995). *La domination masculine*. Paris: Seuil.

Bourdieu, P., and Passeron, J. C. (1970). *La reproduction*. París: Les Éditions de Minuit.

Bruner, J. (1995). *Actos de significado. Más allá de la revolución cognitiva*. Madrid: Alianza (v.o. 1990).

Buendía, L., and Colás, P. (1998). *Investigación educativa*. Sevilla: Alfar.

Bukowski, W., Sippola, L., and Newcomb, A. (2000). Variations in patterns of attraction to same- and other-sex peers during early adolescence. *Developmental Psychology, 36, 2,* 147–154.

Buss, D. (2000). *The dangerous passion: Why jealousy is as necessary as love and sex*. New York: Free Press.

Butler, J. (1999). *Gender trouble. Feminism and the subversion of identity*. New York: Routledge.

Byrne, D. (1971). *The attraction paradigm*. New York: Academic.

Cabrera, F., Espín, J. V., Marín, M. A., and Rodríguez, M. (1990). La formación del profesorado en educación multicultural. In Essomba, M. A. (Coord.), *Construir la escuela la escuela intercultural* (pp. 75–80). Barcelona: Graó.

Carnoy, M., Castells, M., Cohen, S., and Cardoso, F. (1993). *The new global economy in the information age: Reflections on our changing world*. University Park: The Pennsylvania State University Press.

Carr, W., and Kemmis, S. (1988). *Teoría crítica de la enseñanza*. Barcelona: Martínez Roca. (v.o. 1986).

Carter-Scott, C. (1999). *If love is a game, these are the rules: Ten rules for finding love and long-lasting, authentic relationships*. New York: Broadway Books.

Castells, M. (1997). *La era de la información. Economia, sociedad y cultura, Vol. I: La sociedad red*. Madrid. Alianza (v.o. 1996).

Castells, M. (1998a). *La era de la información: Economía, sociedad y cultura, Vol. II: El poder de la identidad*. Madrid: Alianza (v.o. 1997).

Castells, M. (1998b). *La era de la información: Economía, sociedad y cultura, Vol. III: El fin del milenio*. Madrid: Alianza (v.o. 1997).

Castells, M., Flecha, R., Freire, P., Giroux, H., Macedo, D., and Willis, P. (1994). *Nuevas perspectivas críticas en educación*. Barcelona: Paidós.

Catala, A. V., and García, E. (1989). *¿Qué quieres hacer de mayor? O la transición desde la coeducación*. Valencia: Generalitat Valenciana, Consellería de Cultura, Educació i Ciència, Departament de la Dona.

Centro de Investigación y Documentación Educativa. Ministerio de Educación, Cultura y Deporte (CNICE). (2003a). Accessed February 6, 2003 http://www.cnice.mecd.es/.

Centro de Investigación y Documentación Educativa. Ministerio de Educación, Cultura y Deporte (CNICE). (2003b). *Recursos Educativos de apoyo a las enseñanzas de Primarias, Secundaria y Bachillerato*. Accessed February 6, 2003 http://www.cnice.mecd.es/recursos. html.

Chomsky, N. (1997). *Perspectives on power. Reflections on human nature and the social order*. Montreal: Black Rose Books.

Chomsky, N. (2000). *Mantener la chusma a raya*. Tafalla: Txalaparta (v.o. 1994).

Colás, P. (2001). La investigación sobre género en educación: El estado de la cuestión. In Pozo, T., et al. (Coord.), *La investigación educativa: Diversidad y escuela* (pp. 15–33). Granada: Grupo Editorial Universitario.

Cole, M., and Scribner, S. (1982). Consecuencias cognitivas de la educación formal e informal. La necesidad de las nuevas acomodaciones entre e aprendizaje basado en la escuela y las experiencias de aprendizaje de la vida diaria. *Infancia y Aprendizaje, 17*, 13–18.

Comer, J. P., Haynes, N. M., Joyner, E. T., and Ben-Avie, M. (1996). *Rallying the whole village: The Comer Process for Reforming Education*. New York: Teachers College Press.

Comisión de las Comunidades Europeas. (1995). *Libro Blanco: Enseñar y aprender. Hacia la sociedad de conocimiento*. Luxemburg: CECA-CE-CEEA.

Coombs, P. (1985). *La crisis mundial en la educación. Perspectivas actuales*. Madrid: Santillana. (v. o. 1968).

Corneau, G. (1999). *Lessons in love: The transformation of the spirit through intimacy*. New York: H. Holt.

Cosmopolitan. Glattstein Franco, S. (Director). (1998, Agosto, 2003, Julio). *Cosmopolitan*, 8–98 a 6–03. G+J España.

CREA. (1996–1998). *Comunidades de aprendizaje*. Proyecto para la Consejería de Educación del Gobierno Vasco.

CREA. (1998). *Teoría i metodología comunicativa: diàleg i transformació social*. ACES–CIRIT.

CREA. (2001–2003). *Brudila Calli: Las mujeres gitanas contra la exclusión. Superación del absentismo y fracaso escolar de las niñas y adolescentes gitanas*. Plan Nacional de Investigación Científica, Desarrollo e Innovación Tecnológica. Instituto de la Mujer Ministerio de Trabajo y Asuntos Sociales.

CREA. (2002–2003). *Metodología comunicativa del proyecto Workaló*. (Unpublished). Elaboradoen el Workpackage 4 del Proyecto Workaló. *The creation of new occupational patterns for cultural minorities: The Gipsy Case*. RTD Project. 5th Framework Programme. European Commission.

CREA. (2003). *Metodología comunicativa del Proyecto Workaló*. Accessed August 29, 2003 http://www.neskes.net/workalo/Metodog%EDa%pdf.pdf.

Centro de Investigación y Documentación Educativa (CIDE). (2003). Accessed July 24, 2003 http://www.mec.es/cide/.

De Beauvoir, S. (1982). *El segundo sexo*. Buenos Aires: Siglo XX.

Delors, J. (1996). *La educación encierra un tesoro*. Madrid: Santillana. UNESCO.

Deniega, G. (1995). Love is selective. *Russian Education and Society, 37*, 67–84.

Departament D´ensenyament. (1997). *Igualitat d`oportunitats noies i nois. Orientacions per aldesplegament del currículum*. Barcelona: Generalitat de Catalunya.

Departament de la Presidencia – Comissió Interdepartamental de Promoció de la Dona. (1991). *Pla d`actuació del gobern de la Generalitat de Catalunya per a la Igualtatd`oportunitats per les dones: 1989–1992*. Barcelona: Generalitat de Catalunya.

Dewey, J. (1994). *Democracia y educación*. Madrid: Morata (v.o. 1916).

Diez, D. Juárez, O. (Coord.) (1997). *¡De buen rollo! Programa de prevenció de les relacionssexuals no protegides*. (Material audiovisual). (Available in the Institut Municipal de la Salut, Ajuntament de Barcelona (Barcelona City Council), c/ Plaça Lesseps, 1, 08023, Barcelona.

Diputació de Barcelona. (1999). *Pla integral per la Igualtatd `Oportunitats 1998–2002*. Barcelona: Institutd `Edicions de la Diputació de Barcelona.

Dorno, I. (1993). Love is a time of breakdown. *Russian Education and Society, 35*, 67–78.

Dugosh, J. (2000). On predicting relationship satisfaction from jealousy: The moderating effects of love. *Current Research in Social Psychology, 5*, 17, 254–263.

Eco, U. (1992). *Los límites de la interpretación*. Barcelona: Lumen (v.o. 1990).

Eichler, M. (1991). *Nonsexist research methods: A practical guide*. London: Routledge, Chapman and Hall, Inc.

Elboj, C. (2001). *Comunidades de Aprendizaje. Un método de Educación Antirracista en la Sociedad de la Información*. Unpublished doctoral thesis. Departament de Teoria Sociològica, Filosofía del Dret i Metodología de les Ciències Socials. Universitat de Barcelona.

Elboj, C., Puigdellívol, I., Soler, M., and Valls, R. (2002). *Comunidades de aprendizaje. Trasformar la educación*. Barcelona: Graó.

Elster, J. (1996). *Tuercas y tornillos*. Barcelona: Gedisa (v.o. 1989).

Elster, J. (1999). *Alchemies of the mind: Rationality and the emotions*. New York: Cambridge University Press.

Elster, J. (2000). *Strong feelings: Emotion, addiction and human behavior*. Cambridge, MA: MIT Press.

Elster, J. (2001). *La democracia deliberativa*. Barcelona: Gedisa (v.o. 1998).

Epstein, D., and Johnson, R. (2000). *Sexualidades e institución escolar*. Madrid: Morata: (v.o. 1998).

Espín, J. V. (1993). Diferencias de género en la intervención educativa: un tema vigente en investigación. *Revista de Investigación Educativa, 23*, 48–63.

Espín, J. V. (2002). Educación, ciudadanía y género. En Bartolomé, M. (Coord.), *Identidad y ciudadanía. Un reto a la educación intercultural* (pp. 105–129). Madrid: Narcea.

Espín, J. V., et al. (1996). *Análisis de los recursos educativos desde la perspectiva no sexista*. Barcelona: Laertes.

Espín, J. V., et al. (2002). *Anàlisid`estereotips i biaixossexistes a la publicitat*. Informe d`Investigació presentat a l`Institut Català de la Dona, Generalitat de Catalunya. Barcelona: Multicopied document.

Fast, J. (1983). *Sexual chemistry: What it is, how to use it*. New York: M. Evans.

Feminario de Alicante. (1987). *Elementos para una educación no sexista*. Alicante: Víctor Orenga.

Fernández-Peña, L., and Sampedro, V. P. (s.f). *Adolescencia y violencia de género*. Materiales didácticos para la coeducación. Consejería de la presidencia del Instituto asturiano de la mujer. Accessed on November 11, 2014 http://www.prncanst.es/salud/promociones/ESEXUAL/AFECTI-SEXUAL.pdf.

Ferrada, D. (2001). *Currículum crítico comunicativo*. Barcelona: El Roure.

Findler, B. (1995). *Listen up: Voices from the new feminist generation*. Seattle: Seal Press.

Flecha, R. (1990). *La nueva desigualdad cultural*. Barcelona: El Roure.

Flecha, R. (1997). *Compartiendo palabras: El aprendizaje de las personas adultas a través del dialogo*. Barcelona: Paidós.

Flecha, R. (1999). Modern and postmodern racism in Europe: Dialogic approach and antiracist pedagogies. *Harvard Educational Review*, 69, 2, 150–171.

Flecha, R., and Gómez, J. (1995). *Racismo: no, gracias. Ni moderno ni postmoderno*. Barcelona: El Roure.

Flecha, R., and Miquel, V. (2001). Globalización dialógica: Globalización y educación. *Revista de Educación, número extraordinario*, 317–327.

Flecha, R., Gómez, J., and Puigvert, L. (2003). *Contemporary sociological theory*. New York: Peter Lang.

Flecha, R., Puigvert, L., and Ríos, O. (2013). The new masculinities and the overcoming of gender violence. *International and Multidisciplinary Journal of Social Sciences*, 2(1), 88–113.

Font, P. (s.f.). *Educación afectiva y sexual en la escuela. Orientaciones para nuestros maestros*. Instituto de estudios de Sexualidad y de la Pareja. Áreaeducativa: Educaciónafectiva y sexual. Accessed on January 20, 2003 http://www.iesp.info/documents/Educacionsexual.pdf.

Foucault, M. (1987). *Discipline and punish: The birth of the prison*. New York: Random House.

Foucault, M. (1994). *Microfísica del poder*. Barcelona: Planeta Agostini (v.o. 1971–1977).

Foucault, M. (1999). *Estrategia de poder. Obras esenciales, Vol. II*. Barcelona: Paidós (v.o. 1994).

Fraser, N. (1996). *Justice interruptus: Critical reflections on the "postsocialist" condition*. New York: Routledge.

Freire, P. (1970). *Pedagogy of the oppressed*. New York: The Continuum Publishing Company.

Freire, P. (1993). *Pedagogía de la esperanza*. Madrid: Siglo XXI (v.o. 1992).

Freire, P. (1997a). *Pedagogía de la autonomía*. Madrid: Siglo XXI (v.o. 1996).

Freire, P. (1997b). *A la sombra de este árbol*. Barcelona: El Roure. (v.o. 1995).

Freud, S. (1975). *Obras completas*. Madrid: Biblioteca Nueva.

Fromm, E. (1947). *El miedo a la libertad*. Barcelona: Paidós (v.o. 1941).

Fromm, E. (1959). *El arte de amar. Una investigación sobre la naturaleza del amor*. Buenos Aires: Paidós (v.o. 1956).

Fundación Serveis de Cultura Popular. (1997). *Sentir que sí, sentir que no*. (Documentary). (Available in the Fundació Serveis de Cultura Popular, c/Provenca, 324, 2nd floor, 08037, Barcelona).

Garcia, C., and Puigvert, L. (2003). Sociología y currículo. In Fernandez Palomares, F. (Coord.), *Sociología de la Educación* (pp. 262–280). Madrid: Pearson Educación.

Garfinkel, H. (Ed.). (1986). *Ethnomethodological studies of work*. London: Routledge and Keagan Paul.

Generalitat de Catalunya. (2003). *Departamentd `Ensenyament*. Accessed on January 2, 2003 http://www.gencat.es/ense/

Giddens, A. (1986). *The constitution of society: Outline of the theory of structuration*. Cambridge: Polity Press.

Giddens, A. (1989). *Sociology*. Cambridge: Polity Press.

Giddens, A. (1990). *The consequences of modernity*. Stanford: Stanford University Press.

Giddens, A. (1991). *Modernity and self-identity: Self and society in the late modern age*. Stanford: Stanford University Press.

Giddens, A. (1993a). *The transformation of intimacy: Sexuality, love and eroticism in modern societies*. Stanford: Stanford University Press.

Giddens, A. (1993b). *Sociology*. Cambridge: Polity Press (v.o. 1989).

Gilligan, C. (1982). *In a different voice: Psychological theory and women´s development*. Cambridge, MA: Harvard University Press.

Giroux, H. (1990). *Los profesores como intelectuales*. Barcelona: Paidós (v.o. 1988).

Giroux, H. (1997). *Cruzando límites. Trabajadores culturales y políticas educativas*. Barcelona: Paidós (v.o. 1992).

Giroux, H. (1999). Pedagogía crítica como proyecto de profecía ejemplar: cultura y política en el nuevo milenio. In Imbernón, J. (Coord.), *La educación en el siglo XXI. Los retos del futuro inmediato* (pp. 53–62). Barcelona: Graó.

Giroux, H., and Flecha, R. (1992). *Igualdad educativa y diferencia cultural*. Barcelona: El Roure.

Gobierno de Aragón. (2003). *Departamento de Educación, Cultura y Deporte*. Accessed on January 2, 2003 http://www.aragob.es.

Gobierno de Canarias. (2003). *Consejería de Educación, Cultura y Deportes*. Accessed on January 2, 2003 http://www.educa.rcanaria.es.

Goffman, E. (1980). *Estigma. La identidad deteriorada*. Buenos Aires: Amorrortu (v.o. 1963).

Goffman, E. (1981). *La presentación de la persona en la vida cotidiana*. Buenos Aires: Amorrortu (v.o. 1959).

Goleman, D. (1996). *Inteligencia emocional*. Barcelona: Kairós.

Gorrotxategi, M., and de Haro, I. M. (1999). *Materiales didácticos para la prevención de la violencia de género. Educación Secundaria*. Málaga: Consejería de Educación y Ciencia de la Junta de Andalucía.

Gramsci, A. (1976). *La alternativa pedagógica*. Barcelona: Nova Terra (v.o. 1937).

Grandpré, M. (1973). *La coéducation dans les éscoles de 45 pays. Enquête internationale de l`éducation comparée*. Québec-Canadá: Paulines.

Habermas, J. (1987a). *Teoría de la acción comunicativa, Vol. I. Racionalidad de la acción y racionalización social*. Madrid: Taurus (v.o. 1981).

Habermas, J. (1987b). *Teoría de la acción comunicativa, Vol. II. Racionalidad de la acción y racionalización social*. Madrid: Taurus (v.o. 1981).

Habermas, J. (1989). *El discurso filosófico de la modernidad*. Madrid: Taurus (v.o. 1985).

Habermas, J. (1998). *Facticidad y validez*. Madrid: Trotta (v.o. 1992).

Habermas, J. (1999a). *La inclusión del otro*. Barcelona: Paidós (v.o. 1996).

Habermas, J. (1999b). The European nation-state and the pressures of globalization. *New Left Review. The Dark Side of Democracy*, 235, 46–59.

Habermas, J., and Rawls, J. (1998). *Debate sobre el liberalismo político*. Barcelona: Paidós (v.o. 1996).

Hargreaves, A., Earl, L., and Ryan, J. (1999). *Una educación para el cambio: Reinventar la educación de los adolescentes*. Barcelona: Octaedro (v.o. 1996).

Harimaguada. (1994). *Programa de educación sexual*. Canarias: Departamento de Educación. Gobierno de Canarias.

Harris, M. (2000). *Teorías sobre la cultura en la era posmoderna*. Barcelona: Crítica (v.o. 1999).

Izquierdo, M. J. (2000). *Cuando los amores matan*. Madrid: Libertarias.

Jencks, C., and Bane, M. J. (1976). La escuela no es responsable de las desigualdades sociales y no las cambia. In Gras, A., *Sociología de la educación: Textos fundamentales* (pp. 278–287). Madrid: Narcea.

Junta de Andalucía. (2003a). *Red Telemática Educativa de Andalucía*. Consultado el 2 de Enero de 2003 desde http://averroes.cec.junta-andalucia.es/.

Junta de Andalucía. (2003b). *Red Telemática Educativa de Andalucía*. Consultado el 2 de Enero de 2003 desde http://averroes.cec.junta-andalucia.es/contenidos/coeducacion.php3.

Junta de Andalucía. (2003c). *Red Telemática Educativa de Andalucía*. Consultado el 2 de Enero de 2003 desde http://averroes.cec.junta-andalucia.es/publicaciones/valores/mceso_coeducacion.pdf.

Kast, V. (2000). *La naturaleza del amor*. Barcelona: Paidós (v.o. 1984).

Kemper, T., and Reid, M. (1997). Love and liking in the attraction and maintenance phases of long-term relationships. *Social Perspectives on Emotion*, 4, 37–69.

Klein, M., and Riviere, J. (1953). *Love, hate and reparation*. London: Hogarth.

Kohlberg, L. (1981). *Essays on moral development: The philosophy of moral development*. San Francisco: Harper & Row.

Kuhn, T. S. (1975). *La estructura de las revoluciones científicas*. Madrid: Fondo de Cultura Económica (v.o. 1962).

Kymlicka, W. (1996). *Ciudadanía Multicultural. Una teoría liberal de los derechos de las minorías*. Barcelona: Paidós (v.o. 1995).

Kymlicka, W. (1997). *The new debate over minority rights*. Toronto: University of Toronto Press.

Latorre, A. (2003). *La investigación-acción. Conocer y cambiar la práctica educativa*. Barcelona: Graó.

Latorre, A., Del Rincón, D., and Arnal, J. (1996). *Bases metodológicas de la investigación educativa*. Barcelona: Hurtado.

Lee, J. A. (1988). Love-styles. In R. J. Sternberg and M. L. Barnes (Eds.), *The psychology of love* (pp. 38–67). New Haven: Yale University Press.

Levin, H. M. (1998). Accelerated schools: A decade of evolution. In Hargreaves, A., Lieberman, A., Fullan, M., Hopkins, D. (Eds.), *International handbook of educational change: Part two* (pp. 807–830). Norwell, MA: Kluwer Academic Publishers.

Lieberman, C. (1997). *Bad boys: Why we love them, how to live with them, when to leave them.* New York: Dutton.

Lienas, G. (2001). *El diari lila de Carlota.* Barcelona: Empúries.

Lincoln, Y. S., and Guba, E. G. (1985). *Naturalistic inquiry.* Beverly Hills, CA: Sage.

Lomas, C., and Arconada, M. A. (1999). Mujer y publicidad: De la diferencia a la desigualdad. In Lomas, C. (Comp.), *¿Iguales o diferentes? Género, diferencia sexual, lenguaje y educación* (pp. 113–156). Barcelona: Paidós.

Luhmann, N. (1986). *Love as passion: The codification of intimacy.* Cambridge: Harvard University Press (v.o. 1982).

Luhmann, N. (1996). *La ciencia de la sociedad.* México: Anthropos (v.o. 1990).

Luna, F., and Jaussi, M. L. (1998). CP. "Ramón Bajo" de Vistoria-Gasteiz. Una Comunidad de aprendizaje. *Cuadernos de Pedagogía, 270,* 36–44.

Luria, A. R. (1987). *Desarrollo histórico de los procesos cognitivos.* Madrid: Akal (v.o. 1976).

Lyotard, J. F. (1987). *La condición postmoderna.* Madrid: Cátedra (v.o. 1979).

Málik, B., Sánchez, M. F., and Sebastián, A. (2001). *Educar y orientar para la igualdad en razón del género. Perspectiva teórica y propuestas de actuación.* Madrid: Universidad Nacional de Educación a Distancia.

Mandler, G. (1980). The generation of emotion: A psychological theory. In Plutchik, R., and Kellerman, H. (Eds.), *Emotion: Theory, research and experience, vol I. Theories of emotion* (pp. 219–243). New York: Academic Press.

Marín, M. A. (Coord.) (2002). *Buenas prácticas de Educación Intercultural.* Barcelona: Universidad de Barcelona.

Marina, J. A. (2002). *El rompecabezas de la sexualidad.* Barcelona: Anagrama.

Marx, C. (1970). *La contribución crítica de la economía política.* Madrid: Alberto Corazón Editor (v.o. 1920).

Maslow, A. (1975). *Motivación y personalidad.* Barcelona: Sagitario (v.o. 1954).

McDonald, K. (1998). Defining the nature of attraction. *The Chronicle of Higher Education, 44,* 14–15.

Mead, G. H. (1990). *Espíritu, Persona y Sociedad.* México: Paidós (v.o. 1934).

Medina, A. (2002). *Bases teóricas y metodológicas del paradigma comunicativo para la investigación en ciencias sociales. Tesis doctoral inédita.* Departament de Teoría Sociológica, Filosofía del Dret i Metodologia de les Ciències Socials. Universitat de Barcelona.

Merton, R. (1977). *La sociología de la ciencia. Investigaciones teóricas y empíricas.* Madrid: Alianza (v.o. 1973).

Merton, R. (1980). *Teoría y estructuras sociales.* México: Fondo de Cultura Económica (v.o. 1968).

Ministerio de Cultura – Instituto de la Mujer. (1985). *Primeras Jornadas. Mujer y Educación.* Madrid: Serie Documentos, 3.

Ministerio de Cultura – Instituto de la Mujer. (1987a). *La investigación en España sobre Mujer y Educación.* Madrid: Serie Debates, 2.

Ministerio de Cultura – Instituto de la Mujer. (1987b). *Modelos masculino y femenino en los textos de E.G.B.* Madrid: Serie Estudios, 14.

Ministerio de Educación y Ciencia. (1987). *El sexismo en la enseñanza*. Madrid: Serie Coeducación, Colección Documentos y Propuestas de Trabajo.

Ministerio de Educación y Ciencia. (1989). *Libro Blanco de la Reforma del sistema Educativo*. Madrid: autor.

Ministerio de Educación y Cultura. (1990). *Ley Orgánica de Ordenación General del Sistema Educativo*. Madrid: Ministerio de Educación y Ciencia.

Ministerio de Educación y Cultura. (1998). *Catorce años de investigación sobre las desigualdades en educación en España*. Madrid: CIDE.

Ministerio de Educación, Cultura y Deporte (MEC). (2003). Consultado el 6 de Febrero de 2003 desde http://www.mec.es/.

Monereo, M., and Riera, M. (Eds.). (2001). *Porto Alegre. Otro mundo es posible*. Barcelona: El viejo Topo.

Moreno, M. (Coord.) (1992). *Del silencio a la palabra. Coeducación y reforma educativa*. Madrid: Instituto de la Mujer.

Nicholson, L. (1997). *Second wave. A reader in feminist theory*. New York: Routledge.

Nietzsche, F. (1985). *Más allá del bien y del mal*. Madrid: Edaf (v.o. 1886).

Nietzsche, F. (1987). *La genealogía de la moral*. Madrid: Alianza (v.o. 1887).

Norman, J. (1998). *The human sexuality web*. Accessed on August 9, 2001 http://www.umkc. edu/sites/hsw/other/evolution.html.

O.C.D.E. (1987). *La educación de lo femenino: estudio internacional sobre desigualdades entre muchachas y muchachos en la educación*. Barcelona: Aliorna Teoría y Práctica.

Oliveira, M. (1994). *Eros: materiais para pensar o amor*. Vigo: Xerais.

Oliveira, M. (1998). *La educación sentimental: una propuesta para adolescentes*. Barcelona: Icaria.

Oliveira, M. (2000). La educación sentimental. Una carencia en el sistema educativo. En Santos Guerra, M. Á. (Coord.), *El harén pedagógico. Perspectiva de género en la organización escolar* (pp. 71–88). Barcelona: Graó.

Ortega y Gasset, J. (1999). *Estudios sobre el amor*. Barcelona: Óptima (1ª edición Espasa y Calpe, 1964).

Padilla, T., Sánchez, M., Martín, M., and Moreno, E. (1999). Análisis de los estereotipos sexistas en una muestra de estudiantes de CC. De la educación. *Revista de Investigación Educativa, 17*, 1, 127–147.

Parekh, B. (2000). *Rethinking multiculturalism: Cultural diversity and political theory*. New York: Palgrave.

Parsons, T. (1951). *The social system*. London: Routledge & Kegan Paul.

Parsons, T. (1960). *Structure and process in modern societies*. Glencoe, IL: Free Press.

Parsons, T. (1966). *Societies: Evolutionary and comparative perspectives*. Englewood Cliffs, NJ: Prentice-Hall.

Pateman, C. (1988). *The sexual contract*. Cambridge, UK: Polity Press.

Payá, M. (1996). Aproximación a las teorías psicológicas sobre desarrollo moral. *Pensamiento educativo, 18*, 105–136.

Piaget, J. (1968). *Educación e instrucción*. Buenos Aires: Proteo (v.o. 1967).

Piaget, J. (1983). *La psicología de la inteligencia*. Barcelona: Crítica (v.o. 1967).

Piaget, J., and Inhelder, B. (1973). *Psicología del niño*. Madrid: Morsta (v.o. 1969).

Popper, K. R. (1974). *Conocimiento objetivo*. Madrid: Tecnos (v.o. 1972).

Puigdellívol, I. (1998). *La educación especial en la escuela integral. Una perspectiva desde la diversidad*. Barcelona: Graó.

Puigvert, L. (1994). La práctica de un derecho: una alternativa comunicativa al feminismo de la igualdad y la diferencia. *Congreso Internacional Nuevas Perspectivas Críticas en Educación* (pp. 121–127). Barcelona: Fundació Bosch i Gimpera.

Puigvert, L. (2001). *Las otras mujeres*. Barcelona: El Roure.

Pullein-Thompson, C. (1989). *Pare desconegut*. Barcelona: Pòrtic.

Ragazza. Multigner, A. (Directora). (1998, Agosto–2003, Julio). *Ragazza*, 106–165. Hachette Filipacchi, S.A.

Rambla, X., and Tomé, A. (Eds.). (2001). *Contra el sexismo. Coeducación y democracia en la escuela*. Madrid: Síntesis.

Reich, W. (1985). *La revolución sexual: para una estructura del carácter autónomo del hombre*. Barcelona: Planeta (v.o. 1936).

Reich, W. (1995). *Análisis del carácter*. Barcelona: Paidós (v.o. 1993).

Sabariego, M. (2002). *La educación intercultural ante los retos del siglo XX*. Bilbao: Desclée de Brouwer.

Salecl, R. (1998). *(Per)versions of love and hate*. London: Verso.

Sánchez, M. (1999). La Verneda-St. Martí: A school where people dare to dream. *Harvard Educational Review*, 69(3), 320–335.

Santos Guerra, M. Á. (1984). *Coeducar en la Escuela. Por una enseñanza no sexista y liberadora*. Madrid: Zero.

Santos Guerra, M. Á. (Coord.) (2000). *El harén pedagógico. Perspectiva de género en la organización escolar*. Barcelona: Graó.

Sau, V. (1986). *La mujer: el fin de una imagen tradicional*. Barcelona: Icaria.

Savall, A., Molina, M. C., Cabra, J., Sarasíbar, X., and Marías, I. (1997). *Jo, tu i nosaltres (Cos, sexualitat i afectivitat)*. Barcelona: Octaedre.

Schütz, A. (1993). *La construcción significativa del mundo social*. Barcelona: Paidós (v.o. 1932).

Schütz, A., and Luckmann, T. (1977): *Las estructuras del mundo de la vida*. Buenos Aires: Amorrortu (v.o. 1973).

Searle, J. R. (1997). *La construcción de la realidad social*. Barcelona: Paidós (v.o. 1995).

Searle J., and Soler M. (2004). *Lenguaje y Ciencias Sociales. Diálogo entre John Searle y CREA*. Barcelona: El Roure.

Selman, R. (1980). *The growth of interpersonal understanding: Developmental and clinical analyses*. New York: Academic Press.

Seminario Codeases. (1994). Coeducación y educación afectiva y sexual. *Cuadernos de Pedagogía*, 224, 59–64.

Sen, A. (1999). Democracy as a universal value. *Journal of Democracy*, 10(3), 3–17.

Sen, A. (2000). Beyond identity. *The New Republic*, 223(25), 23–30.

Sierra, J. (1997). *Camps de maduixes*. Barcelona: Gran Angular.

Siim, B. (2000). *Gender and citizenship: Politics and agency in France, Britain and Denmark.* Cambridge, UK: Cambridge University Press.

Simón, M. E. (2000). Tiempos y espacios para la coeducación. In Santos Guerra, M. Á. (Coord.), *El harén pedagógico. Perspectiva de género en la organización escolar* (pp. 33–51). Barcelona: Graó.

Skinner, B. F. (1953). *Science and human behavior.* New York: Macmillan.

Skinner, B. F. (1974). *About behaviorism.* New York: Vintage Books.

Slavin, R. E. (1989). *School and classroom organization.* Hillsdale, NJ: Erlbaum Associates.

Slavin, R. E. (1990). *Cooperative learning: Theory, research, and practice.* Englewood Cliffs, NJ: Prentice-Hall.

Solomon, R. L. (1980). The opponent-process theory of acquired motivation: The cost of pleasure and the benefits of pain. *American Psychologist, 35,* 691–712.

Stendhal, M. (1985). *Rojo y negro.* Madrid: Espasa Calpe.

Sternberg, R. J. (1998). *Love is a story: A new theory of relationships.* New York: Oxford University Press.

Sternberg, R. J., and Barnes, M. L. (1988). *The psychology of love.* New Haven: Yale University Press.

Subirats, M. (1997). Notas para la búsqueda de una metodología de cambio desde los estereotipos de género. In Goikoetxea Pierola, J., and García Peña, J., (Coord.), *Ensayos de pedagogía crítica* (pp. 119–126). Madrid: Popular.

Subirats, M. (1998). *Con diferencia: las mujeres frente al reto de la autonomía.* Barcelona: Icaria.

Subirats, M. (1999). Género y escuela. In Lomas, C. (Comp.), *¿Iguales o diferentes? Género, diferencia sexual, lenguaje y educación* (pp. 19–31). Barcelona: Paidós.

Subirats, M., and Brullet, C. (1988). *Rosa y azul. La transición de los géneros en la escuela mixta.* Madrid: Ministerio de Cultura-Instituto de la Mujer.

Subirats, M., and Tomé, A. (1992). *Pautas de observación para el análisis del sexismo en el ámbito educativo.* Barcelona: ICE de la Universitat Autònoma de Barcelona.

Thompson, M. K. (2001). Classrooms for diversity: Rethinking curriculum and pedagogy. In Banks, J. A., and M. Banks, C. A. (Eds.), *Multicultural education: Issues and perspectives* (pp. 152–173). New York: John Wiley and Sons, Inc.

Tomé, A. (1999). Un cambio hacia la coeducación (Instrumentos de reflexión e intervención). In Lomas, C. (Comp.), *¿Iguales o diferentes? Género, diferencia sexual, lenguaje y educación* (pp. 171–198). Barcelona: Paidós.

Tomé, A. (2001). *La investigación-acción coeducativa con el profesorado y las familias.* In Rambla, X, y Tomé, A. (Eds.), *Contra el sexismo. Coeducación y democracia en la escuela* (pp. 85–92). Madrid: Editorial Síntesis.

Touraine, A. (1993). *Crítica de la modernidad.* Madrid: Temas de hoy (v.o. 1992).

Touraine, A. (1997). *Pourrons-nous vivre ensemble?* París: Librairie Arthème Fayard.

Turiel, E. (1984). *El desarrollo del conocimiento social. Moralidad y convención.* Madrid: Debate (v.o. 1983).

Udry, R. (1988). Biological predispositions and social control in adolescent sexual behavior. *American Sociological Review, 53,* 709–722.

Urruzola, M. J. (1995). *Introducción a la filosofía coeducadora*. Bilbao: Maite Canal.

Urruzola, M. J. (1998). *Aprendiendo a mar desde el aula*. Bilbao: Maite Canal.

Urruzola, M. J. (1999). *Educación de las relaciones afectivas y sexuales desde la filosofía coeducadora*. Bilbao: Maite Canal.

Valls, R. (2000). *Comunidades de Aprendizaje. Una práctica educativa de aprendizaje dialogico para la sociedad de la información*. Tesis doctoral inédita, Departament de Teoria i Història del Èducació, Universitat de Barcelona, Barcelona.

Vargas, J. (1999). *Comunidades de aprendizaje. I Jornadas de Cambio Educativo. Teorías practicasque superanlas de sigualdades*. Organized by CREA and held on the 22nd and 23rd of November in the Barcelona Science Park.

Vera, S. (1987). *Los roles femenino y masculino, ¿condicionamiento o biología?* Buenos Aires: Grupo Editor Latinoamericano.

Verena, K. (2000). *La naturaleza del amor*. Barcelona: Paidós (v.o. 1984).

Vergés, O. (1992). *Quincurs el meu tercer!* Barcelona: Cruïla.

Villaescusa, J., and Gorrea, D. (1994). *Coeducación y educación afectivo-sexual*. Cuadernos de Pedagogía, 221, 45–50.

Vygotsky, L. S. (1979). *El desarrollo de los procesos psicológicos superiores*. Barcelona: Crítica. (Edition based on the 1978 U. S. publication. Original articles from 1930 to 1934).

Vygotsky, L. S. (1986). *Pensamiento y Lenguaje*. Buenos Aires: La Pléyade (v.o. 1934).

Weber, M. (1999). *La Ética protestante y el espíritu del capitalismo*. Barcelona: Península. (v.o. 1905).

Wieviorka, M. (1998). Is multiculturalism the solution? *Ethnic and Racial Studies, 21*(5), 881–910.

Xambó, R. (1988). *Sexualitat provisional*. Valencia: Eliseu Climent.

Yela, C., and Sangrador, J. L. (2001). Perception of physical attractiveness throughout loving relationships. *Current Research in Social Psychology, 6*(5), 57–75.

Zurbano, J. L. (2001). *Educación para la convivencia y para la paz: Educación Secundaria Obligatoria*. Pamplona: Gobierno de Navarra. Departamento de Educación y Cultura.

INDEX

TEACHING
✦CONTEMPORARY✦
SCHOLARS

Shirley R. Steinberg
General Editor

This innovative series addresses the pedagogies and thoughts of influential contemporary scholars in diverse fields. Focusing on scholars who have challenged the "normal science," the dominant frameworks of particular disciplines, *Teaching Contemporary Scholars* highlights the work of those who have profoundly influenced the direction of academic work. In a era of great change, this series focuses on the bold thinkers who provide not only insight into the nature of the change but where we should be going in light of the new conditions. Not a festschrift, not a re-interpretation of past work, these books allow the reader a deeper, yet accessible conceptual framework in which to negotiate and expand the work of important thinkers.

For additional information about this series or for the submission of manuscripts, please contact:

Shirley R. Steinberg
c/o Peter Lang Publishing, Inc.
29 Broadway, 18th floor
New York, New York 10006

To order other books in this series, please contact our Customer Service Department:

(800) 770-LANG (within the U.S.)
(212) 647-7706 (outside the U.S.)
(212) 647-7707 FAX

Or browse online by series:

WWW.PETERLANG.COM